LORD, WHAT A FAMILY!

by Robert Hugh Leckie

ILLUSTRATED BY VASILIU

RANDOM HOUSE *New York*

To my wife, Vera,
          who brought to this clan
the thing it lacked and admired most—
serenity.

Contents

LORD, WHAT A FAMILY!

1

*Five Sisters
and Foddy*

"Lord, what a family!" Foddy would shout, and we, according to our guilt or innocence, would quiver, or grin, or vanish softly from the room and dash down to the garage to weather the storm.

It was a classic cry. It rose frequently in our house in Rutherford, New Jersey, and sometimes it might be modified to an angrier bellow of, "Lord, what a lash-up!"—or, if blame could be shifted to Mother, "My Lord, Marion, have you brought a tribe of nincompoops into the world?"

It was usually uttered in dismay, or in mock despair, though sometimes it might even leap heavenward in a sort of grudging gratitude. It was the last prance of the distraught patriarch struggling to preserve authority against the onslaughts of a wife, eight uninhibited children and six unmarried brothers who were disposed to escape the stress of unemployment in the snug harbor at 146 Carmita Avenue. It was also a sound of splendid fury, capable of preserving that order and chilling the hearts of the challengers.

Vocal strength was one of the characteristics of our father, whom we had nicknamed Foddy—perhaps because he scorned and prohibited nicknames. Volume of voice, and power of expression, and fierceness of face—these three. It was the last that was the most awesome, for Foddy had a huge head, which Uncle Tom once described as resembling a squashed pumpkin. His short slender body seemed to exist only to support a paunch and that commanding head. His face was heavily jowled and he had a straight nose and clear, crackling blue eyes. Indoors his head was crowned with a knitted reading cap, suggesting the Pope's *zucchetto,* and outdoors with a wide-brimmed felt affair jammed down to the ears with the brim turned down all around with just enough room to permit the direct glance of those questioning eyes.

Foddy was always questioning. He questioned everyone, except, perhaps, the Almighty, with whom he was in endless supplicating communion. He questioned the staff of the sales and advertising department of a big pencil company, which he ran with brisk efficiency. He questioned the banks which refused to cash the checks that he deliberately made out in pencil, accusing them of collusion with pen companies in perpetuating the myth that a pencil line is not as legal as an ink stroke. He questioned all football officials when the penalty went against Notre Dame. Chiefly, he questioned his daughters, and after that his sons and brothers—and, finally, Mother.

Mother was suspected of secretly encouraging the children to be saucy. Because Foddy went on the road selling, after their marriage in 1906 in Philadelphia, and Mother stayed home, having children, he roared out his half-humorous conclusion: "Marion, by Heaven, these children of yours have been raised behind my back."

5

"A fat lot," Mother would reply haughtily, "that you know about children."

Mother's hauteur and inflexible self-confidence were perfect foils for Foddy's quickness of temper and wit. Where he was angry, she was haughty; where he was scornfully witty, she was tolerantly amused; where he was demanding, she was stiff-backed; and where he was unmistakably the head of the family, she was unquestionably its heart.

Mother was short, too, like all of us. She had a fine brow, and black hair that only four score years would whiten, a straight, strong nose and humorous mouth and a pointed, determined chin. Mother was eight years older than Foddy.

"You robbed the cradle, Mother," we would say, teasing her for one of those long, delightful tales about the men who had courted her before she married Foddy. All of them, it seemed, had been millionaires. But she rejected them, either because she had discovered that they were anticlerical or because they were not "masterful men."

Mother had this habit of exaggeration which also had the power to invest our everyday world with romance. Nothing connected with her family could be commonplace. She could make a simple story of her childhood come alive in the glowing colors of a fairy tale. But she would not boast of anyone in her family, believing, as she said, that "self-praise stinks." Neighbors might find this talent for embroidery somewhat hard to swallow, but it could not be matched for placing a floor beneath the egos of growing children.

Mother sewed constantly. She made many of my clothes and all of my sisters' dresses. Only the Lord can number the pairs of woolen caps and mittens she crocheted. The halls and bedrooms were loaded with the hooked rugs she made of strips of brightly colored cloth cut from worn clothing. She made patchwork quilts, too, and bedspreads and afghans. Her masterpiece was the voluminous reading robe of red-dyed monk's cloth she made for Foddy, which he always wore in the house, and which, with reading cap, gave him the aspect of a sharp-eyed occupant of the Chair of Saint Peter. Though Mother sewed beautifully, she was often defeated in the matter of materials. She could not abide *buying* cloth or yarn. She unraveled old things or cut up others, and it was not unusual to find one of the girls wearing a new dress made of retired curtains, or an exquisitely embroidered bed jacket fashioned from velvet drapes that could no longer keep out the sun.

Both Mother and Foddy enjoyed a joke and encouraged wit and humor among the children—especially the saving capacity for poking fun at oneself. In a large family, it would not do for any single member to develop an inflated estimate of his own importance, and the custom of self-spoofing performs the admirable function of puncturing pretension. It also discomfits selfishness and ridicules that other, and worse, enemy

7

of family harmony, self-pity. Foddy best described the family's special style of humor when the high-school football coach, dropping in one Easter for a mug of egg-nog, remarked on the trait.

"I suppose they come by it naturally, being Irish," he said.

"Yes," Foddy replied sadly, "it's probably unavoidable. You see, the Irish were oppressed for seven hundred years. Having nothing else to do—they decided to get funny."

Unfortunately for Foddy, there were occasions on which his family got funny, in a way not always uproarious to him. This was especially so among the girls, and Foddy often expressed his opinion that whereas incompetent salesmen could be fired and unruly boys beaten, a daughter might only be fed, clothed, endured and despaired of. And he had five of them—petite, vicacious, impulsive and rebellious.

Between my second oldest brother and me there had been an unbroken line of girls: Marion, Catherine, Beatrice, Elizabeth and Madelon. They looked like one another; they thought like one another. They also fought with one another, chiefly because, as they reached full figure, they could wear each other's clothes. But they protected one another as well, and once the last of this quintet had appeared on earth, they banded together in a solid sorority that was Mother's daily trial, Foddy's nightly ordeal and our uncles' unfailing delight. All of them had small faces and straight, pert features and all of them, except Elizabeth, had dark brown hair. Elizabeth's hair, in the family's distaste for mincing words, was described as "dirty blonde." All of them considered Mother their ally, Foddy their master, and me their possession.

This fact was made plain to me when I was about four, when Madelon traded me to a playmate for a doll. I remember quite clearly that I considered this fitting and proper, for Madelon was a year and a half older than I and Foddy's favorite.

Her peculiar standing was a fact of life which everyone in the family accepted with the calm certitude of revelation. Other families might not have favorites, but ours did. It was associated with the Irish tradition of a seventh son. If Foddy should stretch the legend of the fay qualities of a seventh son to include a seventh child—and a daughter at that—it was merely another example of the sorority's power. Actually, there was a seventh son in the family: Uncle Tom. He told me that my grandfather, Patrick Leckie, a Philadelphia businessman, used to make much of him. He took Tom everywhere with him, even to saloons, where the fay Thomas would be the object of awe and admiration. But Thomas became swell-headed. He told my grandmother about the saloons, and was rudely restored to the ranks of his seven other brothers, untouched though they might be by enchanted moonlight. It is an Irish trait to believe in fairies, until they talk too much.

But our Madelon was wiser in that she only fell back upon her standing when in trouble. So I did not quarrel with her right to swap me for a doll stuffed with sawdust.

It was Madelon's first day at the red brick school on Union Avenue. She struck up a deep friendship with a little girl who lived up the street on Carmita. She promised to visit her after class, bringing her little brother along. The friend examined me and said that I was nice. Madelon scrutinized the girl's doll and decided that it was nicer. It was a deal. Madelon went home with the doll, and I stayed behind. The little girl parked me on the front porch, where I sat obediently until the police arrived. Though Mother and Foddy were horrified at the inequality of the transaction, Madelon was quite shaken at the unfairness of a decision which commanded her to return a doll, which was undoubtedly new and hers, and to take back a brother who was getting old and had to be shared with the rest of the family.

The event shook me as well. From it, I could conclude that it was me against the girls. Though Foddy had not surrendered to them, I could expect no help from him, totally engaged as he was in defending his authority against us all. Mother was their covert ally. Much as she might protest impartiality, her actions betrayed the existence of a secret, "most favored nation" pact of the kind diplomats negotiate with the hand that is behind their back while the other is clasped in solemn public friendship with the dupe who has been singled out for subversion.

My brother, John, the oldest child, was an aloof neutral. John had had plenty of time to see the coalition forming and must have decided to get out of the impact area. His policy of neutralism probably had been forced upon him. I had been born too late to be of any help, for I was about fifteen years younger than he—a nearly unbridgeable gap when you are growing up.

My other brother, William, was killed when he was eighteen, and this is the single note of sadness that I will introduce in this book. He had fallen from a moving train against an iron railing and been instantly killed. I was only six then, and my memory of the tragedy was, to me, the strange spectacle of Foddy weeping.

But John, as I say, was a neutral, a noncombatant. He had found the odds too great. His motto seemed to be: if you cain't lick 'em, leave 'em. He acted upon it frequently, moving right out of the house. He would live in a rooming house for a few months, and then return. But another engagement—such as when Catherine kept baiting him at the dinner table by giving him milk when he asked for ketchup—would send him into retreat again.

So I was alone in the field. But rather than retreat, I attacked. With the sweeping magnificence of the six-year-old, I vowed unending war upon all womankind. At the first chance, I seized my mother's scissors and divested myself of those womanish locks—red, in my case —that were then the fashion for little boys. I made certain that although my suits might be of velvet, like Little Lord Fauntleroy's, they would be neither clean nor neat—and soon I tasted triumph in this direction when my sisters came home from school and pretended to their friends that I was someone else's brother.

There were, I found, words which the older neighborhood boys were fond of, and which, when thrown in an uncomprehending fury at the girls, could produce a red-faced rout. You could also strike a terribly confusing blow by refusing to be called "Rob" or "Robin" and insist upon the nickname right of "Bobby."

In disregard of Foddy's prohibition against nicknames, all but John had been tagged with abbreviated diminutives. Marion was Manny, Catherine was Cassie, Beatrice was Betty, Elizabeth was Bobby, from her middle name of Roberta, and Madelon was Madge. When I demanded my name-right, Elizabeth was left with only her proper name. And this, in the marvelously carefree days of the late Twenties—when Black Tuesday had not settled like a shroud on Wall Street, when sticky-sweet nickname names like Candy or Penny had not yet been plucked from the pages of love-story magazines and pasted upon defenseless infants—this was a terrible thing for Elizabeth. She could not claim Betty because Beatrice-Betty, two years her senior, had been there before her and was ready to fight. So poor Elizabeth was stuck with plain

Elizabeth and never forgave me. But it was delicious to have tossed in that apple of discord and to see the sorority rent by schism. It was even better to find that Elizabeth could be goaded speechless by being called "Liz" or "Lizzy." Henry Ford declared that he had made a lady out of Lizzy, but our Elizabeth disagreed.

Name-calling was a tactic that could also be turned against Madelon. By the time I had entered Union School, I had found that Foddy had come close to calling her Maude. Somehow, Madelon had gotten hold of the idea that Maude was a horse's name. In a weak moment of sisterly love, she had confided this to me.

"It's an awful name," she said gravely. "I'm glad Daddy (only Madelon called him Daddy) didn't give it to me."

I nodded in sympathy, and the very first time we quarreled after that—over who should run down to the store—I shouted at her, "Maude! Maude! You've got a horse's name!" She ran to her sisters, leaving me triumphant, though still obliged to get the pound of butter at the A&P.

But she took an awful revenge. It could not have been Madelon alone who designed the counterstroke. It must have been all of them, gathered in Marion and Catherine's room, or assembled behind the bathroom's locked doors—where they customarily convened to take a forbidden smoke or to map out some scheme of concerted action. They remembered me as a singularly damp baby who had kept them flying up and down the stairs for diapers. Remembering, they seized upon it as my Achilles heel.

At the next encounter, as I charged with the ghoulish cry of "Maude, Maude! Maudey the horsey!" upon my lips, Madelon stiffened and countered with the crushing chant: "Mother's Little Water Falls! Mother's Little Water Falls!" The meaning was plain, and I did not tarry to inquire of it. I fled.

Later, perhaps as an unconscious adumbration of F.D.R. and his alphabetical agency-soup, the taunt was abbreviated to "M.L.W.F!—M.L.W.F!" But it never lost its meaning or its power to discomfit, nor was it ever uttered without an exclamation point leaping into place after it in my mind. Not until I was fourteen, when Foddy relented and consented to my putting aside the knickers for long pants, did it disappear.

Nor was it until about a year after they had pointed that horrible shaft that I was able to range myself against them as an independent power. To defend against the girls, I had established a creed and gone into training. The creed was simple: girls are the natural enemy of boys. No non-girl, who has curly hair, a mustache, carries a cane or wears spats, is to be trusted, for he is probably a girl in disguise—a sissy. Sissies do not vanquish girls, therefore it is well to avoid being a sissy and to train as a boy. In the first grade, I had engaged in a few sample bouts, always spurning combat with smaller op-

ponents. I counseled myself that while training for big
things it is not wise to fatten up on small touches. It may
also have been because there were no smaller boys. At
any rate, the tempo was stepped up in the second grade,
and the day that I had disposed of a ferocious third-
grader I considered myself ready.

Betty would be the first opponent. Betty was a tomboy, who had earned glory and her sisters' gratitude by
scattering a bunch of Prospect Place boys who had
barred them from their tree-hut. Well, Betty . . . the
toughest and most valiant . . . batter Betty and the whole
army of the sorority would run for cover in Marion and
Catherine's room, where they could be cornered and
cowed into a tearful and repentant capitulation.

Like Napoleon coming up to Austerlitz, I came up to
the Sunday night ice cream with the sweet savor of victory already on my tongue. Of course, it was I who had
to run down to Miss Meany's for three pints of vanilla-
chocolate-and-strawberry. Of course it was Betty who
dished it out. And of course it was I who got the least.
With the deep, terrifying growl of the seven-year-old,
I attacked.

I got in a good one in what Churchill has immortalized
as "the soft underbelly," drawing up to full height to
deliver this crusher. Betty countered with a movement
of her hips that seemed intended more to save the ice
cream than to stave off destruction. Scrambling erect, I
charged again. Now, they were all shrieking and flailing

15

their arms, all, like Betty, bent on defending the ice cream. But just as I had re-established contact, Foddy entered.

"Lord, what a family!"

"He did it!" they shouted. "He hit Betty!"

"She gypped me on the ice cream," I objected. "She always gyps me, just because I'm a boy!" Foddy glared at all of us and strode over to inspect the size of each helping. I noticed that he wore his suspenders as well as his belt, and since I suspected that the suspenders were for his pants and the belt for me, I decided against over-stating my case. I had been about to suggest a place where girls in general might go. I had been about to hint that they go there immediately, promising to forego my ice cream if that would speed them on their way. But, seeing both belt and suspenders, I let my grievance rest as spoken.

Foddy wheeled on Betty. "Beatrice, give this boy some more ice cream." He turned to me. "And you, young man, don't you ever lay hands on a woman again in your life."

I nodded obediently. Who wanted to, anyway? Hit a girl? Hah! Even Foddy should be able to see that from now on I could subdue any one of them with a fierce look.

2

Mother and the
Mayor of Park Avenue

Midway as the youngest of us were growing up, about 1927, Mother bought a car. She purchased it over Foddy's protests. He told her that he would refuse to learn how to drive it, because the antics of his children had made him too high-strung and the cares of his job too preoccupied. In any case, he added, he detested machinery, and though the times were such that he was forced to use it, he need not become enslaved to it.

Mother said that she would learn to drive. When he replied that she was too old for that, he merely guaranteed his own defeat.

The first car was a Dodge. It was a high, solid, square old horse, with corners rather than curves, and with scratchy upholstery. It was black. All cars were black in those days, except for the sports cars of the very rich—which sometimes rolled elegantly up Union Avenue, provoking, if the rumble seat was occupied by a man and woman, the gleeful shout of "Oh, gee—ain't love grand!"

The Dodge was absolutely not comfortable, but it could contain us and it was serviceable—as were its successors, an Oakland and an Erskine.

It is still a mystery where Mother got the money to buy it, but she did. And though she was by then in her fifties, she had no doubt of her ability to learn to manage it. Once she had done this, she got her license, telling the truth about her age. Later, when it became plain to her that her driver's license was dating her, she adopted the practice of deducting rather than adding a year each time she renewed it.

When she stopped driving at eighty-two, her license said she was fifty.

But she learned to drive, although she was never quite clear about the business of changing gears. Frequently, she covered the first half of a trip in second gear. Foddy would frown.

"Marion, are you quite sure that you know what you're doing?"

"Humph! What would you know about it?"

"But that thing up there—isn't it supposed to be down here?"

At this juncture, Mother's jaw came out, her foot came down on the gas pedal, and the old Dodge leaped forward, still whining in second gear. Only when she had had to stop for a red light, and had to go through the confusing business of shifting gears again, would she covertly slip the gearshift down to the correct place indicated by Foddy.

For as long as she drove, Mother disliked male motorists and carried on unremitting warfare with policemen and bus drivers. Our garage was but ten feet back from Union Avenue, up and down which the big brown New York buses roared. To back out was to enter a no man's land of traffic, but Mother merely placed her hand on the horn, her foot on the gas, and her faith in the Saint Christopher's medal over the dashboard. She darted out of that garage, straddling both lanes of traffic. We closed our eyes while brakes shrieked and bus drivers cursed.

"Mother," we pleaded. "You could get us all killed."

Her jaw would come out, as she sniffed, "Humph! What a pack of yellowbellies."

"But, Mother, supposing the bus driver can't stop?"

"He'll stop."

"But how do you know?"

"I said he'll stop. Now be quiet, will you, while I pass this old thing ahead of us?"

We joked about having received huge offers from the bus company to destroy Mother's license, and also about her skirmishes with a police lieutenant whom we called the Mayor of Park Avenue. He was a brisk, angry-eyed policeman with a weather-beaten face and a trim figure, which was clothed, winter or summer, in blue riding breeches and belted tunic. He gained his nickname from his habit of striding up and down the middle of Park Avenue, the downtown shopping street, to direct traffic. It was his street, dammit, and he ran it with the possessive vigor of a landlord. He had no mercy on women drivers, blaming them shrilly for every traffic tie-up— although, to his credit, he rarely gave a woman a ticket.

Seeing Mother's car approaching, he straddled the white line and placed both hands on his hips. His manner was wary and he frowned his apprehension. Obviously, he would not risk giving her his back for a target. Seeing him, Mother clucked grimly to herself and veered gradually in his direction until she had him squarely in her sights. It was a battle of wills, to see which one would stand the longest or which one would wait the longest before breaking or changing direction. But Mother had the advantage and perhaps the stronger will. Invariably, the Mayor of Park Avenue leaped backward at the last moment and snapped, "Lady, keep to your side of the road!"

"Big bully," Mother would grunt, trying to mask the sparkle of delight in her eye. "I never even so much as touched the white line."

While Mother parked, the Mayor supervised—not to assist, but to make sure that she kept within the law requiring an auto to be within a foot of the curb. But Mother could be content with two feet, or more.

"Lady," the Mayor would growl, "that car ain't parked right."

Mother's reply was always eloquently expressive of her resentment of the domineering male. "Park it yourself then, if you're so good," she would say, tossing him the car keys and stalking off to the shops. For some reason, either because he was secretly baffled by Mother or because he would rather act than argue, if it would keep his street neat and tidy, the Mayor always parked it.

Lord, What a Family!

Without exception, male drivers infuriated Mother. If she drove behind a man, she leaned forward over the wheel eagerly and delivered a running invective at his rear.

"Look at him, look at that old thing, will you? Oh, isn't that just like a man? He didn't even signal!" She would twist the wheel viciously and sweep past the offender, glaring at him past Foddy's nose with a furious disregard for the remaining cars on the road.

"Men!" she would sneer, and Foddy, uneasy, would say, "Please be careful, Marion. Good Lord, you've got your family in this machine."

We took our cue from Mother, winding down the windows to lean out and hoot derisively, "Road hog!" or, "Where'd you get your license—Sears, Roebuck's?" Such unseemly conduct made Foddy shudder. He would throw his hands high in horror whenever one of us began urging Mother, "Pass him! C'mon, Mother, make that slowpoke eat our dust."

At other times, Foddy became sarcastic. If Mother had inadvertently relaxed her foot on the gas pedal, he would say to her, in bittersweet tones, "My goodness, Marion, are we actually under the speed limit?" When Foddy turned around and saw a cat in the back seat, he groaned in disgust. Cats were to be left behind, but they were always being smuggled in.

It is doubtful if we ever pulled away from the house for a ride, without Mother and Foddy already sparring.

First, the food for the picnic was loaded into the car. Then the children. Then Foddy counted us and shook us down for cats. Then he interrogated Mother.

"Have you enough gas, Marion? Enough water? Have you had the brakes checked recently? Where is your driver's license? Are the tires full of air? Beatrice, open the trunk, I want to examine the spare tire. Have the children been to the bathroom?"

Mother would snort, "Will you please get in so I can start the motor?"

"Patience, Marion," came his reply, and then, turning to us, "Robert, is the gas water heater turned off?"

"Yes, sir."

"Who used the kitchen stove last? Elizabeth?"

"Yes, sir. I turned it off."

It was pointless to question us, for he doubted us all. Perhaps he was haunted by the unhappy memory of a recent fire in which Cousin Jimmy, smoking in bed while visiting us, set the mattress ablaze. Invariably, he would turn and re-enter the house. For five minutes, we would wait in the car, fidgeting. Someone would mumble, "What a worry wart," or else, to Mother's delight, begin mimicking him. "Marion, dear, did you bring the steering wheel?" or "Madgie, honey, did you take Snoopy to the bathroom before you put him in the trunk?"

But we were silent, meek, and respectful when he returned. Then, he was off again, trying the front door to be sure that it was locked, circling the house on the lookout for ladders or open cellar windows—while Mother sat hunched in bleak exasperation. At last, he was buttoning his coat preparatory to entering the car, charging us with a final warning against smuggled cats, and then getting in and saying to Mother, "All right, Marion, you may start the motor."

A stutter from the starter, a roar as the motor caught, the snorting of Mother's ejaculation, "Humph, what a man!"—and we were off.

3

Uncles, Ahoy!

We became aware of the Depression when Foddy's brothers began to come to live with us. Until then, the failure of the economy had not meant much to us. We only suspected that something was wrong from the frequency of the hopeless phrase: "Their father's out of work," from the bitter talk about the banks, from a sort of scrip that had been issued to borough employees (notably the teachers), and from the appearance of more and more shabbily dressed men at the back door offering to mow the lawn or clip the hedges for a meal. Drifters would gather at the Erie Railroad Station rotunda. Once as I passed them, one of them called out to me, "Hi, Red," and the rest of them began to joke about what the future held for "red-headed young America." Even then, I could sense the mirthlessness of their humor.

Though Foddy did not lose his job, he became more aloof. He used to sit for a half hour every morning in his chair in the living room. One morning, we heard a loud crash, and rushing in, we saw him standing, white-faced, looking at his chair. A great lump of plaster had fallen in it, just as he was about to sit down. Within a few days, the plaster ceiling was replaced with a metal one, and Foddy moved to the adjoining room, which we called the library. With childish instinct, we connected this event with the Depression and we realized that Foddy sat brooding in his leather chair for a half hour every morning because he was worried.

But when Uncle Hugh moved in with us, we understood that men were not able to get jobs. The fact of unemployment touched on our own lives.

Uncle Hugh was trying to get work in New York, seven miles away across the Jersey meadows. He had studied to be a Jesuit priest, but after twelve years in the Order, he had withdrawn. He had not been ordained. Uncle Hugh was qualified to teach, but there were few enough colleges or universities then expanding their faculties. So he came to live with us while hunting work in New York.

Uncle Hugh was a few years younger than Foddy, who was the next to oldest of their family of eight boys. He resembled him, too, though he was slimmer, and Mother would sometimes insinuate to Foddy that she had thought it was Hugh who was courting her, not John! A detached, professorial manner also distinguished Uncle Hugh, and more than this, a cultivated voice that we kids called "high hat" and a rolled umbrella which he carried in all weather. When Uncle Hugh came home from his fruitless tramping of New York's streets, he would lay down his umbrella in the hall and we would hear his voice raised in that careful, almost lisping inquiry: "Is Poppa home? Do I hear Poppa's voice?"

We would explode with laughter. Elizabeth would chant in a high falsetto, "Is Poppa home?" and Madelon and I would smirk and pipe, "Do I hear Poppa's voice?"

Poor Uncle Hugh, we badgered him without mercy. That mocking refrain of ours must have fortified his resolve to remain a bachelor. Sometimes, in the summer, we would stage a parade while Uncle Hugh sat on the porch reading. Elizabeth would raise his umbrella like a flag, Madelon would shoulder a shovel, and I would pretend that the rake was a rifle.

"Forward, march!" Elizabeth would bark, and we would file away, marching past the chair where Uncle Hugh sat, screaming our battle cry: "Is Poppa home? Do I hear Poppa's voice?"

Five minutes of it would suffice for Uncle Hugh. He would fling down his book, rise and stomp inside the house. There would be the sound of him remonstrating with Foddy, an edge of irritation now plain in that cultivated voice, and we would gleefully dash down to the garage to hide. At last, Uncle Hugh departed. He left, forgetting his umbrella and his degrees, and we never heard from him again except for a letter to Foddy requesting him to forward these cherished objects.

Uncle Hugh was replaced by Uncle Tom, the fey Thomas who had bungled his seventh-sonship. Uncle Tom, too, had studied to be a Jesuit—for eight years. Like his brother, he had not been ordained. Some one of us—I think it was Catherine—invented the tale that Uncle Tom had looked too fondly on the altar wine when it was red, and had been requested to leave. It was not true, of course, but we delighted in it. And, oh, how we delighted in Uncle Tom!

He was taller than Foddy, and handsome in a dark-haired, white-skinned Celtic way. We never saw him angry. His spirits were irrepressible and when the spirits were sometimes liquid, there was no more room for them within him and they bubbled over. He loved to laugh and to tease the girls, but he displayed toward my father an air of respect that was almost filial. There was between them a great gap in age, and it was hard for us to think of Uncle Tom as really being an *uncle*. We thought of him as an older brother, and sometimes even dared to drop the avuncular title and just call him Tom.

Though Tom was able to get newspaper work in New York City, he didn't leave us. He even spread employment around a bit. Elizabeth earned fifty cents a week—paid over solemnly every Friday night—by keeping Uncle Tom's socks darned and clean. It was up to her to separate his from the heap of washed socks that would include Foddy's, John's and mine, and to mend them. Unknown to him, Elizabeth could not sew. But Elizabeth was always resourceful and she intended to keep her job.

Whenever she came across socks of his with holes in them she threw them away and replaced them with an intact pair from Foddy's drawer. Uncle Tom, who thought of clothing as merely something to cover his nakedness—his sartorial appetite was satisfied with the simple dark suit and white shirt which he had worn in the Seminary—was not inclined to examine his socks for anything more than cleanliness and wholeness. If both these conditions were fulfilled, and if they were dark-hued, that contented him, and Elizabeth was careful to filch only dark socks from Foddy's store. But soon, Foddy began to bellow about missing socks.

At the dinner table one evening, his eyes fell on Uncle Tom's ankles. Foddy's eyes narrowed in suspicion. "Thomas," he asked, "whose socks are you wearing?" Elizabeth coughed, requested permission to leave the table, received it, and disappeared. In a moment, the back door slammed.

Uncle Tom answered Foddy's inquiry innocently enough. "Mine, of course."

"Let me look at those socks, Thomas," Foddy growled, rising and stooping to peer at his brother's ankles. His eyes glinted in the joy of recognition, and he roared, "Yes, by Heaven, you're wearing my socks! So you're the one, eh? And does this also explain the dampness of my toothbrush in the morning?"

Uncle Tom shifted uneasily and tried to make light of it. "Don't be ridiculous, John, these are my socks. They were in my drawer this morning. Ask Elizabeth, here . . ." Uncle Tom turned, saw that he was appealing to an empty chair and moved his head in a gentle bob of dawning dismay. He turned back to Foddy. "All right, John, how much did they cost you?"

Elizabeth was fired forthwith.

But not all of Uncle Tom's hired hands were so tricky as she. The quarter which he paid to me every week brought him a full and faithful return. Under the terms of our contract, I was to arise early each morning in the attic room which we shared, seize the bathroom below and hold it for him against the girls.

To execute this assignment, it was required that I stand sleepily outside the door, listening to Foddy washing—mumbling to himself and whooshing as he sloshed water onto his face. Then, when the door was yanked open and he stalked sternly down the hall in his shorts, I darted into the bathroom—just in time to beat Elizabeth bursting out of her bedroom or Catherine racing up the hall in her slip. I would slam the door and lock it. Then I would lie down in front of the radiator to doze until Uncle Tom appeared.

They would raise a furious protest.

"Let me in, let me in. I have to go to work! You don't need to wash yet."

"He's holding it for Uncle Tom. I'm going to tell Foddy!"

"Go ahead, you tattletale!"

"You're a brat! You're nothing but a smart-aleck brat! I know Uncle Tom gives you a quarter for this." Then, in a quieter, coaxing voice: "Come on, Bobby honey, let us in. We'll give you a dime."

"Bribery," I would reply, with conscious pride, "will get you nowhere."

Another storm would break, but then it would subside and I would know that Uncle Tom was outside.

"Uncle Tom, you're terrible. You're making all the girls late!"

I could visualize him grinning at them michievously and I would hear him say, "It's me, kid—let me in." Warily, I would open the door wide enough for Tom to slip by—and then I would slam it shut again and lock it, heedless of the cries of anguish that maneuver had provoked.

When Uncle Tom had finished shaving and washing and had reclothed himself in his bathrobe, he would soak two washcloths in the sink, wring them out slightly, and then, holding one in each hand, say to me, "Okay, kid—open up."

I would unlock the door softly. Swiftly, I would yank it open.

Wham! Whoosh!

More cries. Shrieks of dismay. Slip-clad and hairpinned, they scattered before that washcloth fusillade, while Tom and I ran gleefully down the hall and up the attic stairs.

Once, Uncle Tom armed himself and said, "Okay, kid—open up," and I complied.

Wham! Whoosh!

Silence.

It was Foddy. He was dressed for work.

"Thomas," he said icily, "it is becoming quite clear to me why you left—if you left—the Seminary. But do not flatter yourself with the notion that Saint Ignatius' loss is my gain."

He said nothing to me. He did not need to. From his face, I could conclude that my career as a bathroom commando had ended. I would seize no more early morning beachheads. Thereafter, I earned Uncle Tom's quarters by running down to Miss Meany's for cigarettes or newspapers, or hanging around the telephone in the hall for what seemed hours at a time, waiting to seize the instrument for Tom once it had been relinquished by one of the girls.

But Uncle Tom could never quite down that mischievous passion for slinging things. Nor was he at all choosy in his choice of projectiles. Washcloths or baked potatoes—they were all one to Tom.

We usually had baked potatoes with the Friday night fish. And on Friday night, pay night, Uncle Tom rolled home late. Everyone else would have eaten, but his baked potato and fish would be waiting in the oven.

The moment he entered, I was upon him, badgering him for my quarter, and the girls were clustering around him, begging a forbidden cigarette. He would hand me my quarter. He would hang up his coat and wink at the girls. "You're not supposed to smoke. But if you should remove a cigarette from the pack in my right-hand coat pocket without my seeing you—well, I have not seen you." While they dived for the pocket, Uncle Tom would giggle and stare distastefully at the fish. It was a heartening thing to see Uncle Tom, with his heavy reading in theology, disdaining this penitential staple. When his eye fell upon the potato, he would heft it in his hand and toss it to me with the cry, "Forward pass!"

I would catch it and flip it to Madge. "A lateral." Back it would go to Tom, and he would lean back in his chair and loft me a long high spiral so that I could make a falling, diving catch through the swinging door with his triumphant shout, "Touchdown!" ringing in my ears. The uproar always brought Mother to the dining room.

"Tom, Tom. You're worse than the children. Supposing their father were to walk in here?"

Tom would laugh and push his plate away. Mother never quite understood that Friday night was simply not Uncle Tom's eating night, although it was finally made evident to her the Friday night that he openly refused the fish, and demanded eggs.

Elizabeth scrambled them and placed them before him. She turned and started for the kitchen.

"Hey," Tom called after her. "They aren't done. Here." He raised the plate in the familiar forward-pass motion, as though he were going to toss the eggs to her. He tried not to, I think, but the habit was too strong in him. The eggs slid off the plate and rose in a gentle arc in the direction of Elizabeth. She ducked and then, to our horror, the swinging door opened and Mother entered. It might have been disastrous, had not Elizabeth come through with a stirring interception of that pass. Uncle

Tom rewarded her later with a quarter, and told Mother that it would probably not be necessary to hold Friday night dinners for him any more.

Uncle Tom was also a hot-water thief. He would not go to the cellar to light the gas water heater for his own bath. It is doubtful if he ever went to the cellar, for he had a deep aversion to manual labor and any part of the house associated with toil seemed to depress him. He would not have entered the kitchen, except that the beer was in the icebox there. Uncle Tom usually took his bath after one of the girls had lighted the burner and lain down to nap while the water was heating. He would steal into the bathroom, lock the door and slip into a tub of stolen water. If he was caught, the cries of outrage had no effect on him.

"Uncle Tom! That's my hot water!"

He would snicker and say, "Nonsense, child, you cannot *steal* water. Water is a natural resource which belongs to the people, to everyone—it cannot be stolen."

"That's a lot of baloney. I want my hot water."

"Aw, c'mon, kiddo—you don't need a bath. You hardly smell at all."

"Uncle Tom, you're horrid!"

It was because of Uncle Tom that one of the girls was forever shouting from the head of the stairs, "Somebody turn on the gas water heater!" It was a cry that infuriated Foddy. Hearing it made him bristle, and he

35

would stride into the hall to bellow, "Stop that shouting up there! Come down and do it yourself."

Sometimes his angry eye detected a flash of pink flesh cowering behind the railing, a state of undress resulting from the pleader's anxiety to seize the opportunity presented by the vacant bathtub.

"Have you girls no modesty? Put on your bathrobe this minute!"

At dinner one evening, Betty began to shout from the stairhead. She had eaten early because she had a date, and had hastened upstairs to the bathroom. But all of the hot water was gone.

"Somebody turn on the hot water heater!" she called.

Foddy bent angrily over his plate. None of us moved.

"Somebody turn on the hot water heater!"

Foddy laid down his knife and raised his eyes, transfixing us.

"Marion," he said softly, "if that girl shouts once more, she will not leave this house tonight."

Betty did shout again, but her sentence was never ended. It exploded into a frightened shriek. There was a bumping, scrambling sound and then an ending thump. We leaped from our seats and dashed to the hall.

Overly importunate, Betty had leaned over the rail for the final appeal—and she had leaned too far. But she had not hit the floor. She had fallen between the bookcase and the staircase and had become wedged in there, upside down, unharmed, undressed—but not un-ruffled.

"I'm stuck," Betty wailed. "Somebody get me out!"

"Somebody," Foddy shouted, "get a blanket!"

A blanket was brought and Betty was modestly draped beneath it, like an overturned caryatid, while the rest of us pulled the books from the bookcase. When it was light enough to move, we shoved it away and freed the now giggling Betty.

"Wow!" she said, drawing the blanket around her. "Some entrance, huh? Too bad my date wasn't here to—"

"Beatrice!"

Betty's mouth snapped shut and she fled past him to go down to the cellar to turn on the gas water heater herself.

4

Pirates in
Bathing Suits

It was after Uncle Tom had come to live with us, in the summer of 1930, when I was still nine, that the great event happened. Foddy bought the house at the lake. With Mother's car, we had passed the intervening summers in visits to the seashore or the numerous little lakes lying to the north in the soft green Ramapo Hills. Perhaps Foddy had begun to weary of these week-end ordeals—the packing and unpacking, the long drives in traffic in an automobile loaded with high-spirited children and ruffled cats.

One day in June, Foddy bellowed cheerfully, "Line up, Rutherford!"—his rallying call for the clan—and announced that we were going house-hunting. His first choice was Lake Mohawk, because we had friends there and because a log cabin there was up for sale. The advertisement in the *Times* even spoke of "a brook running through property" and our joy was unspeakable. But we never saw it. Route 23 was just being constructed, and somehow Mother contrived to run the Dodge off the new pavement into the parallel lane, which was a foot below and empty of cement. She couldn't travel on it and she couldn't get the car back up on the proper lane.

We sat there, Mother stewing, Foddy steaming—and crisis following crisis. Someone had to go to the bathroom—"picking daisies" as such woodland ventures were called—Snoopy began meowing plaintively from the trunk, all of the children got hungry, Foddy got a headache, and Madelon began to cry. At last, a construction crew took pity upon us. They helped to get the Dodge back on the smooth going, Mother executed a daring U-turn and we drove back to Rutherford with the front seat enshrouded in silence and the rear filled with children either whimpering or in the full flood of tears.

Foddy vowed never to stir a step from the front porch again, but the next Saturday he drove up to Lake Erskine with John and bought the log cabin.

A log cabin of our own to live in! Dear Lord, what a gift! It was actually constructed of logs—huge, whole chestnut logs, cut and cured before the blight destroyed that beautiful tree in this part of the world. Inside was a big long room which served as both living and dining room, over which hung log rafters suspended from the ceiling. There was a big stone fireplace between this room and the kitchen, a bathroom to the right of the main room with bedrooms on either side, and up above, a rustic balcony for the younger children. A porch ran the length of the front of the house. Best of all, the house was on the lake front.

Moving to the lake for the summer turned out to be a major problem in logistics. The car had to make at least four trips. The first two times, it would be loaded with belongings, with John driving and Uncle Tom alongside on the front seat. John would return alone from the second trip to take aboard more cargo and older children on the third. The Dodge was strictly a passenger liner on its fourth voyage, carrying John, Mother and Foddy, the youngest ones, and, of course, the cats.

When we had all arrived, Foddy rapidly assigned each of us to a station. He and Mother took one bedroom, Marion and Catherine the other, Betty encamped upon the studio couch in the main room, John and Uncle Tom took the porch, and Elizabeth, Madelon and I got the prize—the balcony. It was impossible to sleep that first night. The three of us whispered for hours, unfolding plans for the summer and tasting an anticipatory joy that was almost better than the real thing. We knew that the bathing beach was only a few hundred yards up the road from the cabin, and I was aware that on either side of the house there were boys my own age. At intervals, one or another of us would rise to peer out the window.

"Still dark?"

"Nope, it's getting light."

"Oh, boy!"

Dawn came and, with it, whoops of delight while we leaped from our cots, jumped into our clothes and raced each other downstairs and out the front of the house—stopping short in awe, when, for the first time in our lives, we saw mist rising from water.

Then we came back in and made our breakfasts. That eagerness to be off and outdoors worked as a boon for Mother. She needn't worry about any meal but the main one at evening, for all of us served ourselves in the morning or at noon. But if our impatience was a blessing to her, the popularity of her daughters was a burden.

It did not take long for the word to circulate in Rutherford that the girls had a place at Lake Erskine. Thoughtfully guarding against the possibility of a shortage of young men at the lake, Marion and Catherine and Betty had supplied their friends with our address before we left. When to these were added John's friends, it was no wonder that some Sunday mornings at the lake bore witness to the consumption of four dozen eggs for breakfast.

The vanguard of this hungry horde arrived the very next week end. Within two weeks, Foddy looked despair squarely in the eye, threw up his hands, and howled, "Marion, I have decided what to call this place. We will call it the Halfway House."

They came in flivvers, in rickety roadsters, in ancient, open touring cars that had catchwords daubed on them in white paint, or sometimes the score of Rutherford High School's most recent victory over Passaic. They came without food or toilet articles, frequently without bathing suits—an oversight which any of the girls might correct by lending them Foddy's or Uncle Tom's —and they came to stay for as long as they might until Foddy put them to rout.

They moved in on John and Uncle Tom on the porch and also infiltrated our balcony aerie. Latecomers slept on the front lawn, and it was not uncommon to see them on Sunday morning, rising from the misty earth like soldiers, stretching, strolling to the lake front to douse their faces in water before turning to join the line forming at the kitchen door for breakfast. If it rained, they retreated to the conveyances hopefully called cars.

But Foddy was not a man to ignore the possibility of victory-in-defeat. Like Marshal Foch, attacking with crumbling flanks and collapsing center, he seized upon the biggest, formed them into squads and set them to work with rakes and shovels and paint and brushes. They planted a lawn and tended to it and they also built a retaining wall of stones at the lake shore.

Cousin Harry, brother of the bed-smoking James, was similarly impressed when he came from Philadelphia to stay a week. Foddy saw that Cousin Harry's week was stretching into a week of weeks. He suggested that he spend some of his time building a log fence along the road. With more sagacity than enthusiasm, Harry agreed.

Each morning, he picked up the ax, and with me trotting beside him, trudged off to the woods. Cousin Harry would cut a sapling. I would carry it. It would be deposited alongside the house. Cousin Harry would put away the ax. Within quite a few weeks there were quite a few saplings in a pile.

"Well, young man?" Foddy inquired one morning. "I'm still waiting to see that fence."

Cousin Harry showed Foddy the pile of saplings, explaining, "They have to dry."

"What do you do when they've dried?"

"Peel 'em," Cousin Harry said.

It was by then late August and quite clear that Cousin Harry could be expected back next summer.

To "belong" at Lake Erskine, you had to know how to swim. Of all of us, only John could get around in the water—so my sisters and I had to learn as quickly as possible to preclude being excluded from half of the fun.

The older girls met the requirement with varying degrees of proficiency, but with sufficient skill, at least, to get them out to the raft where the boys were, or to bring them safely ashore should their canoe be overturned. Only the most popular girls ran this delicious risk. If a young lady paddler glided her canoe in close to the raft, and was allowed to pass unmolested, she had better look to her charms. Being dry was no consolation for not being desirable.

We younger ones proceeded with less speed and more genuine interest in swimming. I was nine then, Madelon eleven, and Elizabeth thirteen. We splashed about in the shallow water alongside the big dock. Unfortunately, Elizabeth had heard of the drastic "sink-or-swim" method of instruction. As I sat one day on the dock, over the deep water, she came up behind me and enrolled me in that school. She pushed me in. She laughed when I came up the first time, she called encouragingly when I surfaced on the second—but when the lifeguard plunged in to rescue me before I could take the full count, Elizabeth sprinted for the woods.

After that, Foddy bought the three of us rubber swimming tubes. Within a month, we had learned well enough to leave the rings at home.

Mother availed herself of one of them and entered the lists. Inasmuch as she had learned to drive at the age of fifty-three, teaching herself to swim at fifty-five was no challenge. It was typical of a spirit of curiosity which brought her to sample cigarettes at sixty, and at seventy led her to the martini. Having borne her last child at forty-seven, it was almost as though she were hastening to catch up on the things that she had heard she had missed.

Each afternoon, Mother came down to the beach with her tube slung over her arm. She slipped into it and ventured into the water. We would see her and watch anxiously, for she often paddled in the deep water with a side stroke ineffably her own. When she did, we swam underwater toward her, surfacing beside her, spitting water and cautioning, "Careful, Mother—it's deep out here."

She would snort, " 'Yellowbelly, yellowbelly, can you

swim? Yes, by golly, when the tide comes in!' Of course, I'm all right—I have my tube on, haven't I?"

She did have, but one day she didn't. She had forgotten to put it on, but she thought that she had. When I saw her paddling in the deep water with no support, I jumped in and swam to her side.

"Mother," I said, "are you all right?"

"Humph! You children are too much like your father. Of course, I'm all right. I have my tube on, haven't I?"

"No, Mother, you haven't."

She glanced down, still paddling, and then, with a grin of delight, she said, "Well, think of that! Now I can swim."

Foddy was not so bold in that treacherous element, although he could swim passably with a puffing, stiff-necked breast stroke. He rarely swam during the day, chiefly because he was at work in Jersey City during the week and the beach was too crowded on Saturday and Sunday. He took his dips in the evening, after Mother had driven to the Erie Station in Midvale to pick him up. We always said that he swam at dusk because he was afraid to be seen in that bathing suit of his during the day.

It was an imperial garment. Because only children and young men wore trunks then, Foddy's bathing suit was naturally a one-piece affair covering the entire torso. It was of thick wool, purple below, and broadly striped in violet and white above. Perhaps he chose it because these were the colors of his high school. If so, he was a loyal alumnus.

Although Foddy's bathing suit served him for years, we were forever outgrowing ours. It became expensive to keep us in them, and Mother took to her wool and crocheting needles. The first homemade bathing suit was for me, black trunks of the stiffest, itchiest wool imaginable. I refused to wear them, but Mother said that I would wear them or stay home. I put them on. With misgivings, I walked up to the beach.

"Haw! Lookit the bathing suit he's got. Where'd you get them goofy trunks?"

"My mother made 'em."

"Like fun! She got 'em off a scarecrow."

"Oh, yeah? Can your mother make clothes? Well, then, shut up before I let you have it."

Indignant, now, ready to defend those detestable trunks against all slur, I stalked up to the high board and dived off. It was, I think, a swan dive. I jumped on the board, rose in the air and dropped down. As I entered the water there was a skinning sensation.

I came up with no trunks. The lake had peeled me clean. Treading water, I looked around the surface in desperation. No trunks. I submerged, careful not to arch over in a way that would display what might seem to be a large bald head to that week-end crowd, and searched the bottom. No trunks. I went down a few more times. Mud and stones.

47

Treading water again, I surveyed the situation. There were canoes and rowboats drawn up on the shore, but to get into them I would have to make a Godiva-like dash, with no hope of the modest, eye-shuttered reception accorded that fair lady. Nobody on the shore seemed to be wearing an extra bathing suit. It was too much to expect of friendship to ask a pal to surrender his. I might swim to the raft to hide beneath it until nightfall had sent everyone home. But it was only morning. Even a saint might balk at such a vigil. It was getting more and more imperative that I make up my mind, for swimmers were making sport around me. At any moment I would be found out. When a brace of girl swimmers drifted by, I sank to the bottom in horror and decided to swim home.

I swam breast stroke, fearing again what would happen if I raised my rear into the position required for the Australian crawl. I made a wide circuit around the raft, heading out into the middle of the lake, whence I could veer to my left and swim into the cove where our house was. Halfway out, I heard the lifeguard's whistle. I swam on. It came again in an angry, piercing shrill. Better to sink than be shamed, I thought, and stroked ahead. I could see a few bodies diving into the water to give chase, and I dug my head into the lake and shifted into overhand high.

I got away and reached the cove unmolested. When I had dog-paddled up to our retaining wall, lying spraddled in a few inches of water, I gathered my feet beneath me, leaped the wall and sprinted into the house —as gloriously natural as the day I was born.

Mother was in the main room. I burst in and she looked up calmly, then she became irritable, and suspicious.

"Where are those trunks, young man?"

"I loaned them to a sunfish," I shouted, and raced past her up the balcony stairs.

She thought it not hilarious and she never forgave me for turning up my nose at homemade swimming trunks.

Always, the girls. They were inescapable. Even at the lake—with woods and water for sanctuary—they surrounded you. If it rained, and you were at last chattering with cold from aimlessly paddling the canoe in the downpour, or had taken flight from the lightning flashes leaping over the hills, you came ashore and entered the house and found it filled with girls.

The radio would be on and they would be dancing or just sitting on the benches at the big Dutch table—talking of clothes, boys, and the next dance at the clubhouse on the mountain top. In self-defense, you could go up to the balcony and climb softly out on the railing. Then, like Tarzan of the Apes, you could leap outward and grasp the rafter, swinging backward and forward across the table, to scatter them—refusing to quit until one of them rose and went out to the kichen to make some fudge.

When Foddy had to work late and spend the night in Rutherford, the girls ganged up on Mother for permission to have a party. It had to be a girl party, though: no boys allowed in Foddy's absence. There would be a weenie-roast on the front lawn and the girls would gather—shrieking and chattering away in a most disgusting exhibition of feminine gaiety that soon carried in a mating call over the lake, attracting canoes and rowboats loaded with hungry young hunters. As though by signal, the craft would glide in out of the dusk. They would beach with a scraping sound and then the boys would vault ashore and the girl party would take on the character that the girls had intended for it in the beginning.

Some of those parties were like a foretaste of bliss, sitting there in the soft dark, munching a hot dog and watching the moon rise over the black hills, which seemed to hold the glittering little lake in the hollow of their hands. With the first sight of a faint glow behind the bulk of the hills, someone would shout, "The moon's coming up," and we would wait to see the thick yellow orb poke its topmost curve into view, slowly dragging itself up, up and up from obscurity until at last it stood —round and glowing and benign—in the middle of the summer sky.

At other times, though, the girls ceased to stand for

hot dogs and root beer and beyond-bedtime frolics, and became the symbols of persecution. A boy's ways are not a girl's ways and it was the ironing board rather than the diving board that gave our house its tone. At such times, I would rebel and run away.

"Darn girls!" I would howl. "Have it your own way. I'm leaving! You won't see me around this dump any more."

As though impelled by their derisive laughter, I would slam out of the door and up the walk—the road rising with me, the wind at my back and adventure calling beyond the hills.

It was best to revolt in summer. Though there were a few winter uprisings against the despotism of the sorority—when I would depart Rutherford forever and hitchhike up to the lake, vowing to end my days in that masculine solitude—the hardships of the season were discouraging, and I would either about-face and head homeward, or show little reluctance to return when John and Uncle Tom would overtake me on the road. But on a blue summer day, running away could be a picnic. Naturally, I would be headed for the house in Rutherford—twenty-five miles away.

The first time that I left the lake forever came during a battle with Betty over the ownership of a half dollar. I tore it from her hand, bade the girls a roaring farewell—and hit the road. It was a fine day. It was warm, the birds were singing, the motorists who hastened my flight were kindly, and the fifty cents in my pocket gave me a sense of absolute independence. But it had all been spent on crumb cakes and chocolate milk by the time I walked up Union Avenue and turned in at the back steps. It was getting dark. Somehow, the house did not seem friendly. It was silent and severe.

The doors were locked, but there was always that faulty dining-room window. I reached it by putting one foot in the loop of the water pipe and hoisting myself up. The window gave. I climbed in. The lights did not work, the water did not work, the stove did not work. Nothing worked. It was now too late to gather a few beer bottles and hurry down to Ware's to recoup from bankruptcy. It was too late for anything, except to sit on the stairs in the black, black front hall and hope that perhaps, up there at the lake, they had not taken my declaration of independence too literally.

A piece of cruel despotism from one of the girls would not sit too harshly right now, provided it were committed on a full stomach in the light and laughter of home. I began to think kindly of Betty, wondering if she would weep at my funeral, and I guess that I, too, would have been weeping within a few more minutes if the door had not opened and a flashlight picked me out and the strong arms of John lifted me and carried me out to the car. Foddy was with him. We rode back to the lake in silence, except for the moment when John said, "I don't blame the poor kid. I'd do the same myself with all those skirts around the house."

Foddy seemed not to hear. "I wonder," he said, "if there's a place along the way where we can get something hot to eat."

From this adventure, I had learned the value of being prepared. The next time I provisioned and outfitted myself in advance. Feminine injustice had again appeared, and I was going to shake that cloying dust from my feet.

I made a bindle bag with a stick and one of Madelon's bandannas. In this were placed a few cans of soup (my scout knife with the can-opener blade was in my pocket), a box of Saltines, matches, potatoes, and a half loaf of bread. As an afterthought, I added pencil and paper. There would be regular reports of my progress mailed home to fill them with tearful remorse. I took no toilet articles or pajamas, for I would wash in the rivers and sleep in my clothes, under the stars. Before I left, I borrowed a half dollar from Mother's pocketbook, making a righteous mental promise to repay it once I had made my fortune.

A neighboring woman surprised me at my preparations.

"What have you got there?"

"A bindle bag."

"What's that?"

"That's the bag a tramp carries over his shoulder on a stick."

"My goodness, you're not running away again?"

"I am. I'm through with this dump and all those stupid girls."

"Oh, dear—did you say good-by to your mother?"

The dullness of womenkind was a stupefying thing indeed. Say good-by to Mother! Next, she would want me to disclose my destination. Of this, of course, I was not quite certain. There were the United States Marines and the French Foreign Legion, and there were many cattle ranches in Texas where the bold youth of independent spirit would be welcomed. But this was a later consideration. Now, the thing to do was to be up and off!

"Well, so long. Give the girls the Bronx cheer for me, will you? Heh, heh. Well, so long."

Close-up: bold youth lifts bag to shoulder. Medium shot: walks bravely up walk, refusing to look back. Long shot: walks down road with trees overhead touching branches in silent applause. Fade-out, music up.

Fade-in, music down: bold youth stands on road jerking thumb for rides. Medium shot: cars whizz past. Close-up: bold youth's face, teeth gritted, eyes narrowed, lips drawn back in determination. Zoom out to long shot of car coming down road, stopping, bold youth getting in. Interior shot, car: woman at wheel, bold youth hunched with bindle bag between knees, woman speaks:

"Where are you going?"

"West."

"Who gave you permission?"

Close interior shot, car: bold youth's face, lips parted, eyes wide in disbelief, dismay—bold youth speaks:

"Mother!"

We rode home in laughter, stopping at a road stand for a hot dog and a bottle of root beer.

The biggest apple of discord between the girls and me was the family canoe. I tried to establish squatter's rights in it, but there was always some relative in skirts dashing off to Mother or Foddy in pursuit of a restraining order. When I painted it a brilliant canary yellow it seemed to me that I had put my mark upon it. A ruling from Foddy demolished this piece of chicanery and set up a schedule whereby I had possession in the morning and the girls in the afternoon and evening. I sought to discourage them by hiding the paddles. But they sicked the law on me again.

"Mother, that little brat hid the paddles. Make him tell us where he put them."

Thwarted, there remained only vengeance, which could be taken by rallying my pals to shower the girl-occupied canoe with lumps of mud as it slipped out of the cove's mouth past a little wooded headland, or else soaking the cushions in water just before one of them set out on an evening's ride with a boy friend. Inevitably, such sniping was ruled contempt of court and the girls obtained a total injunction which forced me to construct a craft of my own.

This was an abandoned, water-soaked rowboat which lay a few yards offshore of a little island in the middle of the cove. My pals and I dragged it to our front lawn, hauled it out, set it up on boxes and spent half that summer refurbishing it. We calked it and painted it and built a superstructure on it, and when it was finished, well, there was a sleek and bristling pirate ship and out there beyond the cove—there was the Spanish Main.

We hoisted a ragged Jolly Roger, took aboard a cargo of wooden cutlasses, large clumps of mud for cannon balls, and a board for plank-walking, and set sail.

"Shiver my timbers, mates, she's listing to starboard."

There was a pronounced bias to the right, perhaps because that side of the superstructure was built first and received all of the best wood.

"Avast there, me hearties, hard aport."

Anyone who has been a pirate and knows the lingo will understand Sir Henry Morgan's order to mean sit hard on the left gunwales before we go under. With the crew bravely perched aport, their rear ends half submerged in the water, the ship still listing a bit drunkenly to starboard, the *Jolly Roger* made the mouth of the cove, caught a strong wind and fell in a flaming fury upon the plodding merchantmen and bullion ships moving unsuspectingly over the water.

> *Fifteen men on The Dead Man's Chest—*
> *Yo-ho-ho, and a bottle of rum!*
> *Drink and the devil had done for the rest—*
> *Yo-ho-ho, and a bottle of rum!*

"A sail, skipper!"

"After them, men—and give no quarter!"

The *Jolly Roger* became the scourge of Lake Erskine, with its cruel skipper and ferocious crew. On its first cruise, it bagged six canoes, two rowboats and a kayak—and the shrieks of the womenfolk as they walked the plank, prodded from behind by a wicked-looking cutlass, failed to move the stony hearts of those savage buccaneers.

Within a week, a rival pirate craft appeared on the lake.

"Give 'em a whiff of grape, men!"

The mud-shells arch out from both vessels. *Sper-lunk, sper-lunk.*

"Stand by to repel boarders!"

There is the thrilling clash of steel upon steel, the cries of the wounded—the ships rock dangerously, locked in mortal combat. There is the sound of splintering wood, the enemy is foundering, but the *Jolly Roger* is settling, too.

"She's sinking, skipper!"

"Don't give up the ship, men!"

"Like fun! I'm swimming ashore."

Tanned, half-naked bodies flash outward and plunge into the water. In the middle of the lake, the *Jolly Roger* and the enemy ship disappear below the surface. The battle is over, and so is our career as pirates.

But combat with the rival gang was continued ashore, this time with rubber-band guns in a stone "fort" that lay deep in the woods. A rubber-band gun was a weapon contrived of pieces of wood, and rubber strips cut from old tire tubes. The trigger was usually half of a clothespin, pressed against one end of the wood and held in place by a thick strip of rubber stretched from end to end. Thinner strips—the bullets—were stretched from the front end back to the trigger. You fired by pressing the trigger, which released the rubber strip and sent it twanging toward a charging foeman.

Our fort was truly a stone tower which rose to a dizzying height from the ground. The defenders crouched on top of it to fire down at the attackers, moving in from the woods with bloodcurdling screams. Sometimes they slung their rubber-band guns and climbed trees to snipe at the men in the fort from there. It was warfare of the most merciless kind, and always, defeat or victory depended more on lung power than gun power.

Twang.

"I got you! You're dead!"

"You didn't—you just hit my arm. I'm only wounded."

"Liar!"

"You're another!"

So it went, the fierce clamor of battle, the twanging of the bullets, and the shouted claims of destruction countered by shrill denials with the ensuing exchange of insults—until dusk put an end to the fighting and the weary warriors ran home to dinner.

Usually, we took to the woods when it was too cold to go swimming. If we tired of the sport at the fort, we packed a lunch and hiked to a brook that came twisting and dancing down through trees and ferns. Some times we would dam it up to make a waterfall, or just follow it up to its source in a meadow where daisies grew.

Foddy asked Madelon and me to take him to the brook one Saturday. Foddy was an armchair naturalist. He collected the works of W. H. Hudson, the English stylist and naturalist. We could tell that he had been reading Hudson if we heard some remark such as, "I saw a bunch of wood violets this morning, Marion." We knew that if he had seen them, he saw them from a sidewalk. So we were astonished to hear that he actually wanted to tread the bare earth and risk getting his feet wet.

When we had entered the lane that sloped down to the wooden bridge over the brook, Foddy stopped and picked up a heavy stick. He swished it viciously through the air and whacked it hard against the trunk of a tree. He cried out in pain and cursed and shook his hand.

Madelon said, "What's the stick for, Daddy?"

"Snakes. You must always be on the lookout for serpents when you are walking in the woods."

He swung the stick again with fierce vigor, not, however, against the tree, and we nodded gravely and marched down the lane ahead of him. A snake slithered quickly over the path and disappeared in the underbrush. Foddy halted.

"What was that?"

"Oh, just a garter snake. There's plenty of them around here."

"Are you quite sure that it was not poisonous? How do you know that it was a garter snake?"

"I can tell."

"How far away is this brook of yours?"

"Just down the lane. C'mon, we'll show you."

He tapped his stick uneasily and eyed us with suspicion. Then he said, "What are you children doing in your bathing suits? Don't you know that you can catch poison ivy out in the woods that way?"

"We already had it this summer. C'mon, let's go down to the brook."

Stepping forward gingerly, glancing warily at the spot where the snake had vanished, keeping to the center of the lane, he followed us. When we heard the gurgling of the water, we ran down to the bridge. Foddy came puffing after us. He stopped and looked over the railing.

"Ah, yes. Very sylvan indeed." He closed his eyes and said softly, "I come from haunts of coot and hern." When he opened them, we had disappeared. We had jumped down to the bank of the stream.

"Madelon! Robert! Where are you?"

"Down here. Aren't you coming?"

Though it was a challenge which no admirer of W. H. Hudson could loyally refuse, it was not accepted with eagerness. There was something like sorrow, like a deep wash of self-pity, in his voice when he replied, "Just one moment, children, while I take off my shoes."

We led him upstream. We led him over stepping stones and along muddy banks, through clumps of fern and dead leaves, up a foaming, frothing series of little waterfalls like miniature cascades, tripping over roots or clambering over flat stones slimy with moss—we led him through a green and watery hell, while all the way he fortified a failing resolve with mumbled quotations from *Days in Patagonia* or *The Book of a Naturalist*—quotations which began gaily enough but which became by turns angry, mocking, despairing and at last sardonic. We showed him water bugs gliding over the water, trout darting about the pools, spiders crouching in cobwebs, beetles under rocks, chipmunks scurrying into tree trunks (seeming like rats to him) and, once, in a deep pool, a water snake, and, as a concluding delight at the end of the journey, we wanted to show him the meadow where the daisies grew bright for the picking.

"Mother likes daisies, Daddy—they're her favorite flower."

He looked at his white, white feet spattered with mud, his rolled trousers soaked to the thighs, and he said, "We will buy your mother some when we get back."

"Oh, Daddy!" Madelon wailed. "We can't go back, now. You haven't seen the meadow. I thought you liked nature!"

He spun us around and gave us a starting push. "I have seen the great outdoors, children, and it is my fervent wish that it shall remain there. Forward, march!"

We returned. Thereafter, Foddy looked at nature through the eyes of Hudson, gaining his first-hand observations of the marvels of creation from the comfort of his chair on the front porch, or from the huge wood blazes he built in the fireplace, often on some of the hottest nights of the summer.

Except for that single lapse, Foddy was forever feuding with nature. He distrusted the elements.

One miserable August, when it rained so often that the back lawn lay under water, Foddy became alarmed and told Mother that we would have to return to Rutherford. The newspapers carried daily warnings of the possibility of floods in northern New Jersey, where rivers were swollen and lakes steadily rising.

"This is serious, Marion. Tell the children to begin packing."

"Humph! Who's afraid of a little water?"

"Marion! I have no wish to play Noah's Ark. I have had no communication from the Holy Ghost assuring me that my family will be saved."

"Oh, that voice! If you think I'm going to give the neighbors something to laugh about, you're mistaken. This is my house and I like it here. I'm staying! *I'm* not afraid of a little rain."

Much as Mother wished to avoid giving the neighbors something to laugh about, she was more reluctant to supply them with a sample of Foddy's lung power. His bellow could easily carry across the lake, and the stunning thing about it was that he could form words and sentences—pungent, smoking and clearly distinguishable —while it was booming away in full volume. When Foddy was articulately angry, his voice was like a radio loud-speaker being played at the top of the dial. Mother's final taunt was about to produce that explosive effect. She saw him rock backward on his heels, inflate his chest and open his mouth to roar, and she said quickly, "All right, all right, don't shout. We're going."

We assembled, packed and drove down to Rutherford. It continued to rain for a few more days, but when it had ceased, Mother snorted and said, "How about it, Noah—do you think it's safe to send forth a dove?"

5

"Silence! Your Father Is Speaking!"

During fall, winter and spring, the dining room at 146 Carmita was the heart and center of family life. Everyone had to be present for the evening meal, if only to be counted. The dining-room table—at the head of which sat Foddy, keeping order, inspecting the dishes placed before him, running the silverware through his napkin to detect signs of indifferent dishwashing, correcting table manners—was at once a court of arbitration, a receiving center for complaints and a board of review.

Foddy ruled on such familial cases as whose turn it was to select that night's radio programs or play the phonograph, promised to "look into" reports of broken bedsprings or cold bedrooms, granted requests for permission to sleep at a friend's home or suggested that Mother "do something" about getting "that boy's" hair cut.

Throughout, he strove to preserve at least a semblance of discipline amidst all that exuberant exchanging of jokes or recounting of the day's trials or triumphs. But, sometimes, the girls would rise up in impish rebellion—and he would be forced to "clear the table."

One evening, he glanced up from his plate painfully. He stopped chewing and reached his fingers delicately to his mouth. He drew forth a hair—a beautiful, silken, girlish hair. He held it up to the light of the chandelier. The table fell silent.

"Marion," he said in a strained voice, "would you mind identifying this ingredient for me?"

Mother snorted, "It's a hair, and you know it."

"Whose?"

At once, five girlish voices chanted, "Not mine."

Foddy brandished the hair as though it were Exhibit A in a murder trial. "I want to know whose hair this is."

Marion reached for it hesitantly and examined it. "It isn't mine. My hair's curly and it isn't that light." She looked accusingly at Catherine. "It's yours."

Catherine giggled. "Like fun. Yours is the straight hair. Anyway, I'm doing the dishes tonight. You and Betty helped Mother with the meal."

All eyes, directed by Foddy's, swerved to Betty, sitting between Madge and Elizabeth across the table from Marion and Catherine. I sat next to Mother.

Betty's face reddened. She began to choke. "Maybe," she said, "maybe it's the cat's."

"Beatrice!"

Silence. Then, with a roar:

"LEAVE THE TABLE!"

Her face crinkling with suppressed mirth, Betty arose, placed her knife and fork on her plate, and marched out to the breakfast nook. Her back was eloquent of the laughter that was rising within her, and it was also the signal for the beginning of a parade of departing diners that must have been all too frequent an event for Foddy. It was as though he could not punish one of them without having to penalize them all.

Marion began to hum one of the crooner's tunes then in vogue. "Bub, bub-aboo, bub-aboo."

"No singing at the table!"

"I was humming."

"Leave the table!"

Marion left. A low giggling was audible from behind the swinging door opening on the breakfast nook. Catherine's face became dreamy. She drew a bobby pin from her hair, placed it in her mouth, and began to twist a curl with her fingers.

"That's enough of that! This is not a dressing table."

"Oh, my," she said, her words garbled by the bobby pin clenched in her teeth. "Ain't *that* the truth!"

"Leave the table!"

Now, the choking sounds behind the door were louder and there was an excited buzzing rattle of silverware.

"Quiet in there!"

Elizabeth coughed, forgetting to cover her mouth with her napkin and to turn her head away.

"Leave the table!"

There were now four happy miscreants consigned to the gay unrestraint of the breakfast nook. Madelon began to cry.

"What's wrong, dear?" Foddy said gently.

"I want to eat in the breakfast nook," she sobbed. "You *never* send me in there."

"But you didn't do anything wrong, dear."

She stood up angrily. "I don't care! I'm going!" She picked up her plate and marched defiantly out of the dining room. It had begun to sound like a sorority re-union in the breakfast nook. I sat nervously beside Mother, whose head was bent over her plate. Foddy spoke softly. "Do you find this amusing, Marion?"

Mother quickly put her napkin to her mouth, arose and hurried from the room. Foddy fought a brave battle against his temper. At last, he sighed—a long, quivering, issuing sigh—and pushed his plate to one side.

"Robert," he said, wearily, "will you go in there and tell one of those girls to bring me my coffee?"

Generally, Foddy's authority passed unflouted, and during these times of serenity he would hold forth to us. Because he read constantly, he had considerable information to digest. Because he was no joiner, this congestion might be relieved before only one audience, his family. And this was to our everlasting profit. Those ten- and fifteen-minute soliloquies at the dinner table were master-pieces. Here, in all reality, was Oliver Wendell Holmes's Autocrat. We would hear a discussion of the wine he was drinking or of the splendid lunch he had had that day, why Henry II sent Hugh de Lacy to spy on Strong-bow, what was the proper stroke in a pencil drawing, who was Junius, what was—in his own gloriously free translation—the meaning of the motto, HONI SOIT QUI MAL Y PENSE, inscribed on the Order of the Garter ("Pipe the ants in Molly's pants!"), what had the Spanish ambassador written home of the death of Elizabeth, what ailed the Church in America, why the mud at Valmy saved the French Revolution, what was wrong with modern poetry, why a Shakespearean actor should spit when he declaimed, how superior was the box formation in football as taught by Knute Rockne and played by Notre Dame, what might have happened on the Canadian Border if Lincoln had not been assassinated ("Lord, Marion, we had the generals and we knew the new warfare and Lincoln was angry with England!"), what was the meaning of the Red Hand of the O'Neills, why the papal insignia has crossed keys of gold and silver ("Because it's unique, Marion—you must never cross pure metals.")—and out it would spout in a rich, haphazard cascade. We never doubted the authority of all of this, for Foddy did not merely say a thing. He hurled it at you. It came out in an oration, with assertive thumps on the table, sweeping gestures of the arms and the voice rising shrilly in anger or choking in laughter or rippling in scorn—while his audience was showered with a light mist of saliva. Once, the light fell upon the spray arching from his mouth and I saw a rainbow there.

Sometimes, saying grace, he would tire of the formula, "Bless us O Lord, for these Thy gifts . . ." and toss in a bit of poetry, which we, admiringly, thought to be of his own invention. His favorite "grace" began, "Glory be to God for dappled things," and ended, "Praise Him," after it had passed in a leaping imagery through brinded cows and trout that swim and landscapes plotted and pieced, a most marvelous summation of the bounty on the table. Though he suffered us to continue in the flattering illusion that he had composed this prayer, one of us at last stumbled upon Gerard Manley Hopkins and found that Foddy's "grace" was Hopkins' poem, "Pied Beauty." When challenged and reminded that this was a poem and not a prayer, he growled, "What's the difference?" Nobody answered.

Throughout Foddy's soliloquies, Mother sat at the end of the table keeping order. She acted as a sort of stage director for the show. "Silence, Beatrice, your father is speaking."—"Catherine, stop rattling your knife and fork and listen to your father." Plainly, she regarded my father as a sort of walking compendium, with a dash of William Jennings Bryan thrown in. "Your father is a masterful man," she would tell my sisters, hinting that when the time came for them to choose a husband, the quality of mastery should be paramount in their minds. At other times, when he came home from work, getting off the bus at the corner and striding briskly across the street, she would say to me, "Here comes the little man." Only an insensitive fool would fail to make the inference that Napoleon was a little man, too.

"Silence! Your Father Is Speaking!"

On Sundays and holidays we had memorable breakfasts. Though they were not instructive or hilarious like
the evening meals, or gay like the holiday feasts, they
had a ritualistic quality, a flavor that was associated with
Sunday morning as much as the quiet of Union Avenue
as you walked to Mass. Perhaps this was because they
were served in the dining room rather than in the breakfast nook, and because they were prepared by Foddy.

He rose early and went down to the kitchen, still
wearing his bathrobe and knitted reading cap, which
often served as a sleeping cap, too. We could hear him
slamming the refrigerator door, banging pans on the
stove, beating up the batter for hot cakes—for Foddy did
nothing by stealth. We knew that breakfast was ready
when his voice came roaring up the stairwell: "Good
Lord, haven't you children dressed yet? Come down
here this minute and eat the lovely breakfast I've cooked
for you."

Foddy found it difficult to perform this Sunday morning favor for Mother with anything resembling sweet-
ness or grace. He preferred to discourage the notion that
there dwelt within him an unsuspected streak of kind-
ness—so he would bluster, just as he did every weekday
morning when he had cooked Mother's breakfast for her,
leaving it in the oven and roaring as he went out the
front door, "Marion, you'd better get down here before
that food gets cold." He could not simper, "I hope you
like your breakfast, dear." If he had, we would have
worried for his health.

And we, hearing that summons, would hasten down the stairs to the breakfast nook, knowing how Foddy liked his cooking to be appreciated and eaten while it was hot. Once a dish was placed before you, so sizzling you dared not touch it, a litany of praise commenced.

"How do you like those hot cakes, eh?"

"I haven't tasted them yet."

"Well, be quick about it, will you? They're delicious! How's that, eh?"

"Fine, sir."

"And the *sassage?*"

"Wonderful."

"How's the maple syrup?"

"Delicious."

"The coffee?"

"Excellent."

As though in a delighted amen, he would bob his head and bustle back to the kitchen to feed the next hungry arrival. They were wonderful breakfasts, real Vermont maple syrup on the hot cakes with crisp little brown sausages (Foddy called them "sassage") swimming in a thin gravy, or else thick slices of ham with eggs fried or scrambled or shirred or coddled or poached, or, if you had admired the cooking strenuously enough, scrapple or bacon or kidneys added to the ham. With it all went fresh orange juice, and English muffins dripping in butter, and coffee.

But you had to pass judgment on everything on your

plate. You had to rhapsodize over the hot cakes, salute the sausage, eulogize the ham, venerate Vermont, praise the eggs, ogle the orange juice and sing of the coffee. You could not really begin to eat until you had sampled each variety of the food placed before you and smacked your lips over it. Then, when Foddy had received the only reward he wanted, you started to chew.

Foddy's own breakfasts, once he had done with us, were grilled masterpieces. If there had been hot cakes and sausage for us, Foddy might take this dish as a starter, moving on to a pair of gently basted eggs around which he would reverently stack ham, bacon, kidneys, or scrapple.

He was especially fond of kidneys, often preparing them for himself on Saturday mornings. He slept late Saturdays. Around nine o'clock I would hear a summons from on high, go upstairs and stand beside his bed while he issued his orders.

"Robert, take a dollar from my pocketbook on the bureau and go down to the A&P and get me a kidney and a piece of suet. No nonsense, now, you tell them I want a *good* kidney, a veal kidney for grilling."

"Yes, sir," I would say, steeling myself for a fresh encounter with the butcher. Unknown to Foddy, the man behind the meat counter at the A&P was no admirer of the Leckie clan. He regarded us, particularly me, with sour eyes—probably because he liked to be prepared for the six o'clock quitting time by five o'clock and because Mother had the habit of remembering, at half-past five, something she had forgotten at four. I always had to go down to the butcher's and face that unconcealed displeasure.

Too often, when I ran down on Saturday mornings, faithfully repeating Foddy's injunctions, the butcher would take a small revenge. The kidney would turn out to be the organ of an ancient steer and not the tender, delectable bit of meat that Foddy had requested—and I would be upbraided for a booby and ordered to return and fetch the desired object. But one morning, the butcher growled, "If yer ol' man don't like it, tell him to come down and get it hisself," and I was happy to convey this message to Foddy. Well, he *did* come down, pulling an overcoat over his pajamas and still wearing that cap. He deposited the offending kidney on the counter and said, "You gave my son a beef kidney?"

"Yezzir."

"He asked for a veal kidney?"

"Yezzir."

Foddy silenced his voice and opened up with his eyes, scoring direct hit after direct hit in a way that soon had the target area—the butcher's face—alive with flame, and my own heart aglow with satisfaction. With a mutter of annoyance, the butcher seized his knife, stormed into the storage vault and returned with Foddy's kidney —slapping it angrily down on the scales, wrapping it with exaggerated vigor and handing it over with cultivated bad grace.

"You see, Robert," Foddy said, as we walked back to the house. "You must never let these people face you down."

I nodded, but even then I was vaguely aware that the quality of aplomb which he possessed in great measure was an undoubted gift of nature, either bestowed or withheld at birth, and in no case likely to be acquired. But Foddy thought differently. He was sure that it could be taught.

"Robert," he would say on other mornings, when he prepared to shave, "please take a dollar from my pocketbook on the bureau and get me some razor blades. They are twenty-five cents a packet. When the clerk says a quarter apiece, you say, 'I'll take five for a dollar.'" He would sense my reluctance and add, "Don't be afraid of these people, young man. You'll never get on in business if you let those people bluff you. Tell him that you're a volume buyer and you want a discount. Do you hear?"

"Yes, sir."

I would follow his instructions to the letter, describing myself to the man in the drug store as a volume buyer entitled to a discount, and the affronted druggist would reply by telling me to beat it.

Disappointed by my report of failure, Foddy would lead me back to the store.

"Now, you stand right here, Robert, and watch me." Then, turning with a wink to the druggist as he appeared behind the counter, "How much for one packet of Durham-Duplex?"

"Twenty-five cents, sir."

"Fine, I'll take five for a dollar."

"Yes, sir."

A smile of satisfaction, a wink at me, and we would be out on the sidewalk, with Foddy explaining, "You see, Robert—it's very simple."

Very. To this day, I cannot meet the direct gaze of the man behind the counter.

6

Things A-Brewing

We celebrated four holidays a year: Thanksgiving, Christmas, St. Patrick's Day and Easter. We marked them with gaiety and festive decorations, and, of course, with feasts.

There would be days of preparation. Like an efficient commander on the eve of battle, Foddy would sit down with Mother and draw up a plan of action. Marion would be assigned to the turkey stuffing, Catherine delegated to the mince pie, Betty and Elizabeth ticked off for table duty and perhaps the vegetables, while Madelon and I drew the delightful chore of stuffing the dates, filling them with peanut butter or nuts and rolling them around in sugar.

For days before the big event, Foddy came home burdened with packages. They were wrapped in stiff butcher paper and bound with heavy cord to which little wooden carrying handles had been attached. Such packages were the signature of the downtown New York stores, the Washington Market with its rows of meat stalls and its cheeses piled high in fragrant abundance. When the Erie commuter trains pulled into Rutherford station, and the men swung off with these packages gripped in their hands, it was the harbinger of a party or a holiday feast.

If the big day was Christmas, Foddy brought home

pounds and pounds of candy cane, or toys made of barley candy, all to be hung on the tree. Trimming the tree was always a source of argument, a quarrel which only seniority could decide. It devolved downwards, on the youngest in age, until that method of declining selection settled on me and I was stuck with it for good.

Foddy also brought home five-pound boxes of chocolates and bags of walnuts or cashews or pecans to be heaped in dishes with the silver nutcrackers laid alongside of them. Uncle Tom always promised to bring home ten pounds of chocolates from Schrafft's.

Each Christmas Eve, Uncle Tom came home stricken with remorse. With sad shakes of his head, he would explain that he had left his parcels, forgotten, on his seat on the ferryboat, or else he had been attacked by hoodlums and relieved of both candy and money—and we would collapse in gleeful laughter to hear him tell it.

"Honest, kids, I had just bought the candy and I was walking down Chambers Street, and just then—"

"Thomas!" Foddy would interrupt. "Thomas, did this fantastic event occur before, or after, you had arrived in your present state?"

But there was always a gift for everyone from Uncle Tom and so much candy in the house already that no one really cared. In fact, we came to anticipate Uncle Tom's doleful apologies and we might have been disappointed if he had come home on Christmas Eve with the candy—but no story.

Three or four of Foddy's other bachelor brothers popped over from Philadelphia at Christmas time. There was Uncle Ed, a newspaperman, who always made jokes and grinned and brought us five-dollar gold pieces, which Mother promised to "hold" for us; and Uncle Joe and Uncle Jim, who talked incessantly of horses, much to our bewilderment, for we knew that they didn't ride. Uncle Jim had a cackling laugh and a direct, earthy manner of speech which infuriated Foddy. He talked incessantly of some character he called "Sicky" Smith— "Sicky Smith, kids, he built the world."—and drew endlessly upon a huge stock of Irish jokes which always seemed to single out the parish priest as the butt. Foddy did not consider Uncle Jim a talented comedian. He would rap irritably on the table and say, "James, I am trying to bring up these children to be civilized men and women. Please refrain from introducing barroom humor into this household." But the irrepressible James regarded a rebuke as a compliment, and he always cackled and plunged straight ahead.

Uncle Ed usually arrived a few days before Christmas, to collect the older girls and take them over to a New York night club. Foddy would instruct him to have them safely home before midnight, but they always came clattering home at about two. It was as though they had brought the night club home with them. The front door would burst open to shouts of "Whoopee" or "Ain't we got fun?" and noisemakers would whizz and rattle, horns would blow, paper hats would bob gaily and, with Uncle Ed as conductor and rooter, the girls would begin to sing snatches of the latest Broadway hit tunes they had heard. Foddy would roar down the stairs.

"Edward! Is this a civilized hour for young women to be coming home?"

Uncle Ed's answer was always the same: "I don't know about the time, John, but that's sure some tribe of gold diggers you saddled me with."

At Thanksgiving, the first thing that our family did was to go to the Rutherford-Passaic football game. Not to have seen that game was a social error pardoned only by the plea of impending death. It was the second oldest high school football rivalry in New Jersey, and for those who live in our town, "going to the game" was an especially pleasant holiday sport in that it usually ended in a Rutherford victory. The high school team was then the scourge of New Jersey, the best in the state. The night before the game there would be a huge bonfire and pep rally behind the high school, and the night after the game, if Rutherford had won, snake dances of victory throughout the streets. A visit was paid to the home of each player on the team, and there, gathered in the chill dark of late November, with a raw hint of winter already in the air, with the torches flickering and glinting off the brass buttons of the uniformed bandsmen, and the breath of the happy victors making puffs of vapor in the air, the proud young gridiron gladiator would be called out to the front porch and there cheered by name and by brassy blares from the band. Once, while we were eating Thanksgiving dinner, John was summoned out to his reward, and when the cheers rose lustily into the night I felt an almost unbearable pride. It was as though Red Grange himself were a member of the family.

St. Patrick's Day was another gay time. There would be corned beef and cabbage, and vegetables turned a bright and emerald green by baking soda, green paper hats to be worn and green streamers dangling from the dining-room ceiling, green ice-box cake and green beer, and later, green *crème de menthe* to be sipped. We listened to Irish records, too. As we grew older, the St. Patrick's Day parties became popular with our friends. Those bold enough to tease "the Pope"—my father—appeared in orange ties or hats, which seemed to delight him, much to the astonishment of the timid, who had expected to see him seize a shillelagh and drive the rash, synthetic "Orangemen" into the street.

But they were disappointed, and as for a shillelagh, no such vulgar instrument would have been permitted in the house. Foddy had nothing but a scathing scorn for this club, which, in the popular mind, symbolizes the Irish love of combat. "No gentleman would be caught dead with a thing like that in his hand," he would say.

Nor could he escape the impishness of his blood.

When the St. Patrick's Day guests were predominantly of Irish extraction, he would remember his Scots ancestors and heap scorn upon the Celt. Suddenly, with no regard for the consistency which he regarded as the "hobgoblin of little minds," he would start bellowing about "The Forty-five" and the right of his family to wear a Stuart tartan. The wail of the pipes would come skirling from the record player to the tune of "The Bonnets of Bonny Dundee," or "Cock of the Walk," or "The Renfrewe Gathering," and he would sing and jig in time to it. Once, his suspenders broke and his trousers fell swiftly to the floor. With superb aplomb, he reached down, never losing a step or a note, and pulled them up.

Conversely, when the company was heavily non-Irish, that is to say Scots or Welsh or sprung from that other race, the English, he was a Celt of the Celts. There would be dark allusions to Cromwell and Drogheda, and some unsuspecting listener would be startled to hear Foddy, certainly no Anglophobe, roaring out, "There is nothing Hitler or Stalin have done that the English did not invent and put into practice in Ireland!"

Even during Prohibition there was always some sort of bottled spirits available to make the parties gayer. Our parents were far from being heavy drinkers, yet, like so many Americans, they bitterly resented the Noble Experiment which turned a Puritanical thumbs-down on the wine that gladdens the heart of man.

There was always a bottle or two of wine on the table for the big holiday dinners, to be drunk by the adults, John, and the older girls like Marion and Catherine. The younger ones might beg a sip or two, but the only sure way of discovering the power of the grape was to sneak back into the dining room after dinner to drain the empty bottles and the wineglasses left standing on the table. But there was never enough left over for us to arrive at any really conclusive decision, much as we might pretend that there had been.

During the Prohibition years, John brewed his own beer in the basement laundry. In those days, groceries and delicatessens had shelves loaded with cans of malt and hops. There were even specialty stores devoted to the supply of the necessary equipment: bottles, caps and spidery little capping machines, malt and hops, big galvanized tubs for cooking up the stuff, funnels for bottling—even blank gummed labels for the more dedicated among the amateur brewers who might wish to gain a small local fame.

John and his friends in the Melrose A. C.—a semi-pro athletic group which played baseball in the summer and brewed beer in the winter—would set to work in the laundry, cooking the mixture on the little old iron gas stove Mother used to boil clothes on before the days of the washing machine. We were forbidden the laundry at such times, but naturally we managed to watch the show, usually by going outside and peering in the cellar windows. It seemed an injustice to us that all of this wonderful equipment could not be used for the making of root beer. But it was always lager beer—foaming, frothy, Powerful Beer—that was funneled into the dark green bottles, which were left standing on shelves in the cellar.

In bed at night, we could hear the detonation of the bottles. Sometimes, if the Melrose boys had cooked up a singularly exuberant mess, the bottles would go off with the rapidity of machine-gun fire and we would lie in bed, giggling. In my imagination, I could envision the same thing happening in dark, damp basements all over America: the caps blowing off and the amber fluid spouting ceilingward, defiant geysers cocking a derisive liquid snook at the Eighteenth Amendment.

Easter meant eggnog. Easter eggnog is a Philadelphia custom which my family imported to Rutherford when they moved there in January of 1921. The making of it was a ritual, beginning with a frantic exhortation as Foddy dashed about the house hunting for his recipe. When he had found it, exactly where he had placed it the preceding Easter, there were the extra quarts of milk and the pints of heavy cream to be ordered from the milkman. One of the girls would grind the nutmeg. An additional two dozen eggs were needed from the A&P. Most important, the rum and brandy had to be procured.

With all the ingredients on the table in the breakfast nook, I would be summoned and armed with a big ladle.

Foddy stationed me alongside a two-gallon, cream-colored bowl. His recipe, written in faded pencil on a paper frayed and tattered by years of folding and re-folding, was carefully smoothed out on a tea cart. An apron was around his middle.

"You understand, Robert, you are to stir."

"Yes, sir."

Synchronize your watches, gentlemen, we are about to lay down a preparatory bombardment of sugar and eggs.

In they go. I mash them to a yellow paste.

"Now the milk and cream, Robert."

"Yes, sir."

Gentlemen, the assault has begun.

In go the milk and the cream, and around comes my ladle with the care of a Rembrandt wielding a brush.

"Rum and brandy, Robert."

"Yes, sir."

Charge!

There it is, the brownish liquid making tan streaks in the mixture as the ladle goes round and round and folds it in. Foddy bends over the bowl, gently pouring, his eyes fastened warily on the stirrer as though ready to detect any undue rise or fall of speed in the steady cir-cling of that spoon. Then, the final order:

"Taste it, Robert."

"Yes, sir."

"How does it taste, Robert? Too much rum, too much brandy?"

"No, sir. Very good, sir. You can't taste anything—only eggnog."

"Excellent, Robert—an intelligent criticism."

Victory!

7

Labor Omnia Vincit—

or, "Robert, Fix the Furnace!"

Only a well-organized labor corps could cope with the work entailed in keeping a large house clean and a large family clothed and fed. Mother could not do it all, and during the Depression years, such relief as she had gotten from people like old Mary, who came in during the day, was no longer available. Foddy, of course, helped where he could. But none of us, least of all Mother, would have been other than horrified to see him scrubbing floors or washing windows. In those days, the male parents were fathers. They had not yet become Mommy's lovable mule or the kiddies' playful servant.

So we were divided into labor squads. All of the girls helped with the housework. Marion and Catherine were detailed to assist in the cooking while Betty and Elizabeth cleared the table and washed the dishes. John handled strenuous chores such as putting up screens, thoughtfully aided by Uncle Tom, who shouted encouragement or opened beer bottles for him when he became thirsty and took a break. Madelon and I were supposed to run errands, though we probably expended more energy arguing over who had run the last one. I was also pressed into service as a sort of reluctant utility man in the cellar and the yard.

Much of the time spent in housecleaning was channeled into picking up bobby pins. The house seemed

sown with them. It was not wise to grasp the glass in
the bathroom to rinse your mouth, without first making
sure if it contained bobby pins. Places in books were
marked with bobby pins. They lay rusting on the bathroom porcelain, or atop the piano or the buffet or bookcases. They got into your bed. Walking barefooted
down the hall to the bathroom, you could feel them un-
derfoot at night. Sheets of homework were clasped together by bobby pins. Household articles that sagged or
came undone or fell apart were repaired by them. If
other men worked to keep their families fed and shel-
tered, Foddy shouted importunately at his salesmen in
order to keep his daughters in bobby pins.

In a lesser way, the housecleaners were also kept busy
picking up silk stockings. It was rare to find towels instead of silk stockings on the bathroom towel racks.
Every radiator seemed to blossom with drying silk—and
if the doorbell should ring and the visitor turn out to be
an adult who might possibly stand on propriety, there
would be a mad dash from room to room and a wild
harvesting of those dangling, dripping slips of gossamer.

The food brigade operated smoothly enough, so long
as Marion and Catherine kept their hair up, but the
dining-room crew was perhaps too eager and impulsive.
Betty was always straining to be done and out of the
house. Once she had eaten her own meal, she arose and
began sweeping the table bare. You had to fend her off
with one hand while finishing your food with the other.

Leave a plate unguarded or shift your gaze from a dish, and Betty would swoop down upon it with swift, scraping fork or eager, emptying hand.

Frequently, Foddy was called from the table by a long-distance business call. We could hear him shouting over the telephone. Mother would shake her head and say, "How anyone could work for that man!" Unobserved, Betty would see her chance and move in, and when Foddy would return to the table he would find that he had been given short shrift.

"Where is my food? Where is that girl? Do I have to give her a tip to let me finish my meal?"

Elizabeth had the patience to wait for everyone to finish. But when she began, she started in high gear. She was gay and wisecracking and forever in a bustling hurry. She picked up dishes like the football pass receiver who turns to run before he has quite caught the ball. Elizabeth would reach for a plate, whirl, toss a quip over her shoulder, and sprint for the kitchen—turning in dismay when the sound of breaking china suggested that she had fumbled. She fumbled frequently. In fact, she was at last prohibited from handling china. Is it fair, I wonder, to suspect Elizabeth of deliberately dropping the ball?

Too often, the girls slyly sloughed their work off on the youngest member of the family. Madelon had the faculty of persuading me that I could do a thing more rapidly and skillfully than she, fortifying this with the

hint: "I'll ask Daddy to give you a dime for the movies."
I was also a sucker for the extra dessert:

"Bobby, I'll let you have my chocolate pudding if you
do the dishes for me tonight."

"Peel the potatoes for me, Bobby, and you can have
my piece of pie."

So there I would stand at seven o'clock at night, three
or four desserts straining uncomfortably within me, the
delicious moments of devouring them now but a sad
memory, and a disarray of dishes to be stacked, scraped,
washed, dried, and put away.

"I don't believe it," I would mutter. "I don't believe
Adam got so much as one lousy bite out of that apple."

The girls had other ways of sharing the work. The
home of a big family always seems to attract the neighborhood children, and with five girls in our house, it was
inevitable that by post-dinner time the place should have
the aspect of a secular convent. The visitors arrived just
as the table was to be cleared and the dishes to be done—
and they were eager to get upstairs to Marion and Catherine's room to puff on a surreptitious cigarette or listen
to Bing Crosby on the radio, or, infinitely more pressing,
far, far more vital, just talk about cute fellows.

Thus impatient, they did not object when a towel
was flipped to them, or a load of dishes shoved into their
hands. Obviously, if they did not pitch in, they would
be too late to hear Bing sob soulfully about what happens when the blue of the night meets the gold of the
day.

"Someone waits for me," Bing would sing, and seeing their rapt faces, I would dredge up a disgusted "Yeah!"

It perplexed me, too, why the singing idol of the teen-agers should be sponsored by a cigar company.

As the outside man, most of my labor was directed by Mother. It was up to me to shovel the snow or mow the lawn, rake the leaves, trim the hedges, and help her in her garden. Mother loved roses. The back yard was dotted with rose bushes and there were many trellises, built by Mother with more hope than skill, sagging beneath their load of heavy blossoms. Mother had emphatic opinions about growing roses. She insisted that horse manure could not be matched for fertilizer.

Unhappily, we had no horses and therefore no sources of supply. But there were the dray horses that pulled the bakery and milk trucks. The drivers of these carts always stopped to rest their beasts at the intersection of Carmita and Union, directly in front of our house. When they had flicked their reins and shouted, "Giddyap!" and the horses had wearily clop-clopped away, there would be a bright pile of smoking fertilizer left on the pavement.

"Robert!" Mother would call. "Robert, quick! Get the dustpan."

Her summons provoked a wailing reply. "I'm not going to! You can't make me. You can't make me go out there and scoop up those horse apples in front of all the kids coming home from school!"

"Horse apples, indeed! It's fertilizer I want. Now you go right out there and get it for me."

"I won't! The kids'll all make fun of me."

"Humph! That's the trouble with you city children. Soft and sissified! What's wrong with getting fertilizer for your mother's roses? Now you go out there and get it before the cars run over it. I'll give you a nickel for every dustpan-full you get."

The thing to do was to walk out with the dustpan dangling inconspicuously by your side; then, to stand in an attitude of boredom beside the prized pile, yawning to deceive the youthful passers-by of your intentions, but always being careful to force oncoming cars away from the goal; and then, when the street was deserted, to stoop swiftly, scatter the birds, scoop the stuff up, and race back to the rose gardens. If waiting had made you late for school, Mother could be coerced into writing an explanatory note by the threat of telling all to the sister.

"All right, don't write me a note. I'll just say, 'Sister, the reason I'm late is because I had to pick horse apples for my mother's roses.'"

"Young man!"

But the note and the nickel were always forthcoming, and Mother's roses bloomed bright and fragrant. So did those of a new neighbor we had acquired on Union Avenue, a woman equally fond of roses and convinced as well of the efficacy of horse manure. There came to be red-faced contests between me and this woman's daughter—who later became my wife—over possession of the prize, nor could I comprehend her doggedness until I discovered that her mother had offered her, and any neighborhood kid, an entire dime for a dustpan-full. Mother complained angrily of this irrational price war.

Foddy's interest in Mother's garden was chiefly academic. He might read in the back yard occasionally, or, wearing underwear shorts with magnificent disdain for the effect this might have upon the neighbors, he might stroll outside to make a cursory inspection of Mother's roses. He complimented her on them and he talked grandly of the flora which he had seen in the pages of W. H. Hudson, but he was not one to plunge his fingers into the good, brown earth.

One summer, unbidden, I turned over the back yard and began to plant a lawn. I heard Foddy bellow from the sleeping porch, "Madelon, come here and look. Robert is making a *plaisance!*"

But Foddy was intensely interested in keeping the cellar clean and the fire burning in the furnace, and because half of me was also the cellar man, this portion of my labor belonged to him. It must have been a happy day in his life when he perceived that I was strong enough to heft a shovel-full of coal, or to help him hoist a loaded ash can up the cellar steps. He had been doing it for years, and now, at last, I would understand with what crushing dejection he must have received that report—"The fire's gone out,"—on those nights when he came home from work tired and hungry.

I hated that fire and the furnace that held it. It stood between me and my freedom, or so I thought, with my natural talent for exaggerating the burden of ten minutes' work. It kept me at home when I wished to be away and it got me out of bed when I wanted to sleep.

From October until May thereafter, I had to bank it every night at eleven o'clock and bring it up every morning at half-past six. Though I managed the first dutifully enough, I was completely remiss on the second. I never awoke unless Foddy called me.

Every morning until I was eighteen, when Foddy installed an iron fireman, I awoke to the bellow of "Robbb-bert!" Though it would be winter, and the windows would be closed, the neighbors could hear that alarm. It was as regular and clear as the single clang that sounded seven o'clock every evening in the West End fire-bell tower. But it differed in that it came frequently, and would at last be concluded in a single splendid command.

"Robert-fix-the-furnace!"

So I would grope awake and stumble down to the cellar to minister to that squat, ugly, inhuman brute of a furnace—spitting at it in useless anger, striking it with the coal shovel and slamming the door shut with all my strength. It even drove me to the desperation of verse.

One Christmas, after two years of fuming at the furnace, I left a rhymed summary of my grievances under the tree for Foddy. It said:

When I awake in the morning,
It is not of my own accord.
The reason, dear friends, is my Father
Our Master and Overlord.

At six o'clock in the morning,
When the cocks have started to crow,
His rasping voice, it bids me rise
And down to the cellar go!

So I toss aside my bedclothes,
And walking as though in a daze,
Descend to a dusky cellar
To fix that cursed blaze.

Now, I still believe in Santa Claus
And each day my wish becomes firmer,
That he'll bring to me a fine surprise
In the shape of an oil burner!

Foddy read it, admired it, cautioned me against abuse of poetic license, alluded gently to the Depression, and asked me if I had cleaned out the ash pit.

8

Kid Wolf, Suh,
Soldiah of Misfohtune

Girls, girls, girls. You walked into a room, and it was filled with girls. You went to the bathroom and there was a girl in it. You wanted to make a telephone call, and the instrument had a girl attached to it. You tried to go to bed, and there was a girl in it—and though this may have been an intriguing shock in later years, as I grew up it only reminded me that the enemy had me completely surrounded.

Only through the reading of books could the girls be escaped. This was a hint that I had taken from Foddy. As Mother said, he always had his nose in a book, sitting in his leather chair with the cap jammed down on his head and his body swathed in his robe.

But I could see that Foddy's books could be used as a barricade against the girls. So I made the dining room my sanctuary. No girls came there, it savored too much of work. So I would curl up next to the radiator—where Mother's bread was rising, with that warm yeasty smell—and read.

There were so many books in the house that only the bathroom did not have a bookcase. Mother was not amused when I suggested that she install a short-story shelf in there. But all of the other rooms had bookcases and there were more than a thousand volumes. I know, because I had to count them.

Lord, What a Family!

It was a chore which came to me one rainy Saturday when Foddy paused in front of the hall bookcase and observed that it was overloaded. He peered at some of the volumes and called to me, "Robert, come here and help me rid this bookcase of your Mother's mid-Victorian novels. Phew, what inspiring stuff—'Did-She-Fall-or-Was-She-Pushed?'" After that was done, he assigned me to dusting and rearranging all of the books in the house, promising me a quarter for doing it. I felt almost overpaid, until the job lasted to dinner time and I realized that the bargain had not been mine. That was how I came to count them, and also how I came to regard Foddy's taste with doubts.

Most of the volumes were his—highly stuffy stuff, I thought. There were row on row of voluminous works such as Motley's *Rise of the Dutch Republic*, Gibbon's *Decline and Fall of the Roman Empire*, *The Federalist Papers*, and American histories by Parkman, or English ones—by Lingard and Belloc—Macaulay, Carlyle, Ruskin, Lord Chesterfield, Johnson and Boswell, Taine, and on, and on, and on—a perfectly wretched array of windy guys.

Two of the bookcases were kept under lock and key. One was a dark wood, glass-enclosed case in the living room, loaded with poetry and classics. In there, as I grew older and found the key, I tasted such forbidden fruit as *Moll Flanders*. The other stood in the hall. It was much bigger, and when I found *its* key, I came upon a grove of apple trees. There was Rabelais, and Voltaire's *Candide*, the *Autobiography* of Benvenuto Cellini, and a life of that other interesting character— François Villon—and most entertaining of all, the *Droll Stories* of Balzac. I had never suspected that these windy guys could write so well. Of course, I read many of these too soon to understand them—but they had been sealed off, so naturally they had to be looked at.

For the most part, when escaping the girls, I shied away from Foddy's stuff. There were the Boy Allies and Garry Grayson, with his Winning Kick, Winning Run, Winning Pass, Winning Hit, Catch, Pitch, Shot, Punch, Slide, Stroke, Tackle (how his creator could wrench a whole book out of a single muscular reflex!)— the Rover Boys, of course, and Tom Swift hurtling all over creation in trains, electric runabouts and airplanes. If Tom Swift's author had not run out of gas we would certainly have seen the time of *Tom Swift and His Hydrogen Bomb,* or *Tom Swift and Sputnik.*

But even Tom seemed tame once I had discovered pulp magazines. And the pulps, of course, were forbidden. Foddy extended to the pulps the same disdain which he accorded the Sunday funny papers. When the comics were banned, Foddy offered to take Madelon and me to the Saturday matinees at the Rivoli as a substitute. We went once. Foddy emerged from the theater, holding his ears, quite shaken by "The Blonde Bandit" and the enthusiasm of the audience. "Madelon," he said, "did you actually enjoy this?" "You bet, Daddy. I only had to duck under the seat twice." Foddy shuddered, and we lost his company at the matinees—though we did not really lose the comics, thanks to a kind man across the street who kept huge stacks of them in his cellar just for us.

But the pulps? No!

"They are vulgar, Robert. No child of mine shall be exposed to that sensational bilge. Read something good. Why don't you try James Fenimore Cooper?"

I would have liked to reply, "James Fenimore Cooper, my Lord!"—for I had sampled some of that dreary verbiage. I used to wonder if Cooper had been paid by the pound. For my money, Natty Bumppo wasn't a bump on Kid Wolf's behind. Kid Wolf, suh, soldiah of misfohtune. He had that knife sewn in a sheath behind his neck, and when Slade'd get the drop on him and growl, "Reach for the sky!" old Kid Wolf's hands'd come up and the right one would fasten on that knife, and *Zing!*, that would be the end of Slade. Kid Wolf. *There* was a character.

Vulgar, sensational bilge that they were, I had at least fifty of these thrilling literary masterpieces under my bed in the attic and used to swap them with the neighborhood kids. I got them down at Miss Meany's. She always kept the pulps stacked in neat, gaudy rows on her magazine shelves—westerns, detectives, sports, adventure. There were horror and love stories, too, though the first bored, and the second sickened me. You paid from a dime to fifteen cents for them. Those published by the Street & Smith chain were my favorites.

The pulps were finally drowned in a wave of prosperity and bogus education. So many magazine readers nowadays are college men and women that the publishers have had to raise the standards and give them "mature westerns." What is a mature western? A friend of mine, who wrote the pulps and now does the matures, explained to me: "A mature western is when you pronounce your i-n-g's and the guy kisses the gal." Well, let 'em have their boudoir cowpokes, I'll take Kid Wolf and Slade.

One of the difficulties in getting the pulps at Miss Meany's was her insistence on being paid for them. Depression children rarely had spending money, and the pennies I could get by cashing in beer and soda bottles at Ware's weren't going to keep me in green leaf's *and* the pulps. You couldn't clip the green leaf's. They were safely behind glass in the penny candy counter, along with the "chances" Miss Meany sold. You bought a chocolate cream for a penny and broke it open. If it was pink inside, you won two cents' worth of candy besides. If it was white, you said "Aw, nuts," or brought down some similar imprecation on the luck of the draw, and stuffed it in your mouth. We always swore Miss Meany ran a crooked wheel. We suspected her of removing all the pink creams from the box.

At any rate, the pulps were out in the open—probably because it would never occur to her that anyone would want to steal a magazine. She might insist, "Snap your fingers," when we lounged by the tables stacked with rubber balls or nickel rockets or water pistols, but she ignored us when we strayed over to the magazine shelves. It was simply done. I had a big, blue jacket that I wore. It was called a "hood" because of the cowl at the back, like a monk's, that was pulled over your head when it got cold. My hood came down to my knees, even though it was the smallest my mother could buy. But it looked just like those worn by the high school football players, so I swagger-staggered around in it. It was a simple matter to stand with back to Miss Meany and stuff a pulp up under the front of the hood. You held it there with your hands stuck down in the big patch pockets. Then you turned around to stare absent-mindedly at Miss Meany, and then you strolled out the door.

But beyond the bamboozling of Miss Meany lay the far more perilous undertaking of smuggling a pulp magazine into the house. To do this, I shoved it beneath my inner sweater, hoping to get it past Foddy should I meet him in the front hall. Like Pavlov's dog with the bell, Foddy had a reflex connected with the sound of the front door opening. Open the door and there was the inquiry, "Who is that?" Close it with the reply, "Robert," and there he was, opening the living-room door and sweeping you with his eyes, a book pressed against his chest. I think he surveyed the girls for signs of dalliance—mussed hair or smudged lipstick—and me for the marks of combat—black eye, torn shirt or bruised knuckles. Whatever the reason, he would be there—capped and robed, the blue eyes glittering like Chesterton's Father Brown's.

One night, puffed up by success and overcome by greed, I selected two fat westerns from Miss Meany's racks.

The warm flat feel of them was against my chest as I opened the front door, gave the password, and prepared to run the gantlet. Foddy stood in the doorway and raked me with his eyes. With uneasy nonchalance, I went to the hall closet, removed my hood and hung it up. A quick glance at my bulging sweater suggested to me that I would never make it. In the dark of the closet, I fumbled with the magazines, hoping to leave them there and sneak back for them unobserved. A very clever ruse, worthy of the great Kid Wolf.

"Robert!"

Ah, well, even Kid Wolf had never had to deal with such an hombre.

"What do you have under your sweater?"

"Magazines, sir."

"Give them to me."

I handed over the pulps and presented my ear, and we marched down to the cellar. We came to a snappy halt in front of the coal furnace and the pressure on my ear was withdrawn as he flung open the furnace door and stepped back. Heat rolled out and I gazed miserably at the bed of orange-glowing coals. He shook the magazines at me, and said, "This, young man, is the only fit receptacle for what you mistakenly describe as 'magazines.' Eh? Do you hear that, Robert?"

Faintly, with a spectacular lack of enthusiasm, came my reply, "Yes, sir."

He threw them in. They caught fire immediately. There was just time to see the cover illustration of Kid Wolf firing from a galloping horse, his hair and his buckskin fringes flying in the breeze, and the title, "Six Guns Bark at Rattlesnake Gulch," and then it had curled up and puffed into flame.

"I must admit that they burn very well, Robert," he said. He smiled to himself, and I could guess that he was rehearsing the account, with which he would regale Mother, of how Robert had been caught smuggling literary dope into the house and of how the contraband had been consigned to the flames. Then he barked, "Put two shovels full of pea coal on the fire, Robert, bank it—and go to bed."

Tenderly, I shoveled Kid Wolf under.

The girls also were subjected to Foddy's scrutiny of their reading matter. Once, Catherine and Marion had gotten hold of Thorne Smith's *Turnabout*—a lurid and ludicrous account of what happened when a man and wife swapped sexes. They were reading it aloud in their room. Giggling and muffled shrieks pricked my curiosity and I entered. Madelon, Elizabeth and Betty were on the bed, their legs tucked under them, while Catherine sat next to one window and Marion in front of another. Marion was reading. All of them were smoking.

"Aha!" I said. "Smoking!" The situation showed excellent possibilities for blackmail.

Betty sneered, "I suppose you're going to run and tell Foddy." She held her cigarette just as Clara Bow does it in the movies.

"A nickel seals my lips forever," I replied.

Betty countered with a threat to blow the whistle on me in the matter of a letter from school, which she had showed me how to steam open, though I had needed no instruction in how to destroy it. I changed the subject. "What're you reading? Let me listen, too."

"Beat it," Betty said. "You're too young."

Catherine said, "I'll give you a nickel if you sit at the head of the stairs and play 'chickie' for Foddy."

It was a deal, but as I turned to take up my station, I realized that it had come too late. The door flew open and he strode in. Betty choked and swallowed a mouthful of smoke. Catherine quietly let her cigarette fall out the open window behind her. Marion leaned forward as though to cover the book with her arms, and while Elizabeth and Madelon bumped heads in an effort to hide behind one another, I backed softly out of the door. I heard a single, roaring command, "Give me that book!" and I retreated further up the hall.

Foddy came boiling out of the room with the book in his hands and clattered down the stairs. I heard him making for the cellar. I followed, at a safe distance. I saw him rush up to the furnace, seize the door and fling it open and then step back as though to sling the book inside. He paused. He glanced curiously at the book he held. He opened it and began to read. He read for five minutes, holding the book low, just above his knees, to catch the dim light of the coal fire. Then he chuckled. He chuckled again. He snapped the book shut, slammed the furnace door and marched upstairs. He got his overcoat and hat from the hall closet, put them on and went out the front door. I thought he was going to return the book to the lending library. But, instead, he sat in a porch chair, switched on the lamp and read for two hours.

I can still see him there, his shoulders hunched against the cold, reading *Turnabout*, and his belly shaking with silent laughter. Next day, it was restored to Marion with the order to return it to the library immediately.

"Tripe!" Foddy bellowed. "Unmitigated tripe!"

Marion took it back, reading it on the way.

Books and the discussion of them were almost the single substance of entertainment in our house. Of course, we played card games like Go-Fish or War, or checkers and backgammon and that marvelous game, Monopoly. The man who invented Monopoly deserves a special medal in his honor. We played it for hours, gathered around the dining-room table munching ginger snaps and sipping cider, gravely passing the toy money back and forth while we bought and sold property, went broke or landed in jail. But reading was the chief pastime, and we delighted in talking about our books.

We had a game based upon reading which we called, "Who Said That?" Madelon and I played it in the breakfast nook, quoting—or misquoting—from books and flinging out the inquiring challenge, "Who said that?" The object was to identify the book and author. We played it on even terms, until Madelon pulled poetry on me. She learned it from Foddy, who was fond of reading verse to her. Foddy had a deep and genuine love of poetry, especially the works of the English lake poets. He would call Madelon up to his room to read it to her. He always read poetry aloud, even in the bathroom. We could hear the voice behind the bathroom door murmuring, " 'The moon doth with delight look 'round her when the heavens are bare.' " Then, perhaps, the sound of Foddy gargling, which he did frequently and with gusto, and the voice continuing, " 'Waters on a starry night are beautiful and fair.' "

It was from him that we took our love of reading, in whatever measure we still possess it, and it was the one thing that he most encouraged in us. Always at Christmas, Foddy's gift was a book. Anyone who expressed interest in a book would be sure to receive it, if not bought, at least borrowed from the Jersey City or New York libraries. Naturally, we had many of A. A. Milne's books—from which Foddy got the idea for a Winnie the Pooh Pencil Box. On the frequent Saturdays when Foddy took Madelon and me to New York—to see the marionette shows or visit the old Aquarium or the zoo— we would drop in at the book stores on Fourth Avenue or pay a call at his favorite bookseller's, Mendoza's, on Anne Street. At other times, we would accompany him to the printing houses on Long Island, where he did business, and have printing and the mysteries of the silk screen process explained to us. Foddy also tried to sharpen the curiosity of our minds on these excursions, pointing to buildings in the downtown skyline as we crossed the Hudson on the ferry, identifying them for us, and then, on the succeeding Saturday's crossing, rewarding us with a nickel for each building remembered and named.

I can regard it as a blessing, now, that some of Foddy's books were able to wean me off my beloved pulps and give me a taste of real wine. There was Bulfinch's *Mythology*, and even Kid Wolf never rode a griffin or hunted unicorns. There was a marvelous book of Greek mythology, the title of which I have forgotten, that was filled with warring gods, and there were the Knights of

the Round Table or the Paladins of Charlemagne with
the terrible sadness of Roland at Roncesvalles, and next
a bit of elfin gold called *Irish Fairy Tales*, and more
clashing of steel and working of spells in a little green-
and-gold volume entitled *Battles and Enchantments*,
which told of the druids and the Tuatha De Dannan, the
Fir Bolg and the Melasians and the great Irish warrior,
Lugh. James Stephens, too, with the thin woman of
Innis Magrath whirling off to her grave, and the splendid fairy army gathering for the Rising of the Shee at
the conclusion of *The Pot of Gold*. Who would forget
T. H. White's *The Sword in the Stone*, once he has met
the Wart and heard Merlyn berate the owl atop his wiz-
ard's cap for befouling his soup, or seen bold King Pell-
inore go bounding off after the Questing Beast, or
watched breathless that ferocious battle of magic between Merlyn and the evil sorcerer who had studied at
the university for black magic under the sea? It was all
magic, conjured up from the pages of Foddy's books.
Novels, history, philosophy might follow from this
habit, yet, if I must choose, let me remember the dying
Robin Hood, leaning out the window to shoot that last
sad arrow, rather than Raskolnikov reaching for the horrible ax beneath his coat.

Foddy's fondness for literary allusion could soften an
impending chastisement. Once, caught coming home
well after the deadline, I furnished him with a lengthy
and lurid excuse. I had discovered that he considered an

undistinguished lie almost as culpable as the offense it sought to conceal. I had found that he could be staggered by original falsehood, if it were richly embroidered in detail and leaping with imagery. I served up a beauty. He listened to me intently, and when I had finished, he stepped back a bit and regarded me with amazement.

"My Lord, Robert," he said softly. "You should have been in Boccaccio."

It was the accolade, and, of course, it had the inevitable but undesired effect. *The Decameron,* I told myself standing proudly in the dark upstairs hall, was another book I was going to read, once I found the key to the hall bookcase.

9

Get That Guy in
the Red Pants!

For such a large family, we had amazingly little sickness. Of course there were colds and the grippe and sore throats, and many, many imaginary ailments artfully assumed on the mornings of Test Days in school, but there was a minimum of real illness. The poet William Carlos Williams, who was also our family doctor, used to say to Mother, "Mrs. Leckie, you have the healthiest family in town." Her explanation was simply that a woman with seven children on her hands had little time to pamper them. Her remedies were castor oil and large applications of mustard plaster, tea-and-toast, hot lemonade and, most effective of all, a threat to keep the sufferer in bed over the week end.

Yet, anyone actually sick could expect considerable attention. Meals would be brought on trays and there was always someone about to come and read to you or play Monopoly or checkers on your bed. Foddy was especially attentive to a sick child, always looking in on the patient as soon as he had come home from work. He would bring tea-and-toast or hot lemonade upstairs and stand in the doorway of the sickroom, obviously worried and determined to be gentle, but also struggling not to be too sticky with this sympathy business.

"How do you feel?"

"Fine."

"Hah! Have you had a bowel movement?"

"Yes, sir."

Another glower of commiseration, another "Hah!" and he would stride away, perhaps returning later with a dish of ice cream and a second inquiry about the state of your bowels. Mother and Foddy had great faith in the efficacy of moving bowels. They showed greatest concern when they had discovered that organ to be delinquent, and would dash off to the medicine cabinet in the bathroom, where milk of magnesia and cascara sagrada were kept in plentiful supply among the king-size bottle of mercurochrome and boxes of gauze and adhesive tape. It was a rewarding sight to approach Foddy with a report of the movement of someone's balky bowels, and to see the expression of satisfaction on his face.

The family's robust health seemed proof even against childhood sicknesses such as mumps or measles or whooping cough or chicken pox. I never had any of them, and few of my sisters contracted more than one of them. Once, Elizabeth and Betty had the mumps. Mother, with the resolution born of despair, promptly shoved Madelon and me into bed with them, hoping that we would oblige by coming down with the affliction, too.

"Get it over with," she said to old Mary. "Better to take care of four at a time, than to bother with the little ones later."

It was warm and companionable in the bed, great fun to have the food brought to us and to play cards on the bedspread. Madelon and I hated to leave. When Mary came upstairs to inspect us, we puffed out our cheeks like squirrels and looked at her mournfully. She clucked with pleasure and returned downstairs.

"They've got it, Mrs. Leckie."

With the skepticism of the old hand with children, Mother came up to make a personal examination. We were ready with inflated cheeks. She reached out and pinched them with thumb and forefinger. They collapsed. She sighed wearily.

"Out of there, you two, and get your clothes on."

There was only one occasion when one of us was seriously sick. That was the winter when Madelon had diphtheria. The house was placed in quarantine. None of us was allowed to visit Madelon. Her room was kept dark. For days, there was no laughter in the house, only a hushed quiet. No one spoke to Mother or Foddy unless spoken to. We all went about our chores with a grave efficiency, and the evening meal was eaten in silence.

Then, the crisis passed and we learned that Madelon was recovering.

The sound of voices could be heard again. We were allowed to go in to talk to Madge, who was quite proud of the celebrity which diphtheria had given her, and also the object of envy for the amount of ice cream she was being fed. An enterprising visitor to the sickroom might come armed with a spoon.

"Bobby, you're taking all the chocolate."

"Boy, I wish I'd had diphtheria—look at all the ice cream you're getting."

"I almost died—did you know that?"

"Boy!"

"I could have gone blind, too—the doctor said so."

"Holy smokes! Okay, if I just eat the strawberry?"

But a great event such as Madelon's defeat of diphtheria could not come to an end in our house in a gentle, graduated manner. We required gusto—brass and kettle-drums—and it was the overly efficient Beatrice who supplied the Wagnerian climax. We were at the dinner table. Though Madelon was almost well, she was still in bed. Catherine complained that the dining room was hot. Foddy stopped talking. Mother said she thought that it was rather warm herself, and arose to lay a hand on the radiator. "Why," she said, "the radiator's cold."

Foddy glanced at the radiator, perplexed. Then, a terrible thought struck him. He leaped from his chair, flung open the cellar door and dashed downstairs. We heard him bellow. "I'll say it's hot! Call the fire department! The cellar's on fire."

Mother called the fire department. Next, with magnificent calm, she ordered all of the children to get into their outdoor clothes. John raced upstairs to swaddle Madelon and carry her out in the dark. In a few minutes, the fire engines came clanging up from the West End firehouse, only three blocks below us on Union Avenue, and booted and helmeted volunteer firemen rushed fiercely up the steps, brandishing wicked-looking fire axes.

"Don't you dare break anything," Mother shouted at them. "You go right down the cellar and don't disturb a thing."

Mother's admonition had a chastening effect on the firemen. They slowed their pace and took a shorter grip on their axes. Their backs were eloquent of their disappointment at having been deprived of half the joy in a volunteer fireman's life.

Spectators had gathered outside the house and I could hear a teen-age girl saying, "But when does it burst into flames?" Marion and Catherine were the center of an excited group of high school girls, discussing the likelihood of having to sleep overnight at someone else's house, not without a certain note of hope in their voices. Madelon lay quiescent in John's arms. But Betty was not excited or alarmed. She was apprehensive. "Oh, boy, am I going to get it," she said to Elizabeth.

Mother heard her, and asked, "Why, Beatrice?"

She burst into tears and wailed, "I just remembered where I put the porch blinds."

"Where?"

"Against the furnace."

That, of course, was what had happened. The rolled

blinds, made of bamboo and dry from months in the sun, had been ignited by the heat of the furnace. When Foddy clattered downstairs, he had been confronted by a merry blaze that made it appear as though the entire cellar were alight. But the fire was put out in half an hour, the crowd was dispersed, including the disappointed girl, and we trooped back into the house to finish dinner. Betty was so tearful and so upset by the lurid descriptions of possible punishments supplied her by the bloodthirsty Elizabeth that Foddy took pity on her and waited for two days before giving her "a good talking to." A week later, Madelon was well again and back among us, the glory of her ordeal thrown into brighter relief by the flames of Betty's fire.

Though we were healthy, we were often the casualty of our own high spirits and robust bodies. Broken bones, cuts, bruises, sprains and concussions were common. It was a rare time of tranquility indeed that saw no one's arm in a sling, no leg encased in plaster, no head picturesquely swathed in bandages.

Much of this could be ascribed to the absence of any degree of locomotion in the house other than full tilt. Only Mother walked up the stairs. The rest of us, led by Foddy, dashed up and down them. If the doorbell rang or the telephone jangled, it was as though a starting gun had been sounded. From every corner of the house came the sound of pelting feet, and from the stairway the familiar clatter and bump of someone who had leaped too exuberantly to the challenge of being the first to open the door or answer the telephone. Elizabeth skimmed down the stairs so rapidly one day that she could not make the necessary leftward turn at the bottom and sailed through the porch window, shattering the glass but never her aplomb. Many a visitor was astonished at the speed with which our front door would be flung open, and then was literally taken aback by the storm of hurrying bodies which came hurtling into the hall.

Once, as the telephone in the hall rang, I came rushing down the stairs only to go crashing down the last flight to end with my right foot twisted painfully beneath me. Foddy stormed into the hall, seeking the author of that unseemly racket, but then, seeing me injured, he ran to my side to examine my ankle, probing with an assurance rivaled only by his ignorance of anatomy.

"Lord!" he roared. "This boy's broken his foot!" Then he wheeled and bounded up the stairs to get his coat, shouting over his shoulder that he was going to take me to the doctor's. On his return, he paused at the head of the stairs to bellow down at those gathering around me, "Can no one in this house learn to *walk* down the stairs? Have I fathered a tribe of kangaroos?" As though to answer the last question in the affirmative, he came clattering down again. Forgetful of his diagnosis, he helped me to my feet and bustled me out the front door ahead of him. He led me to the corner where we would wait for the bus. As we stood there, I suggested timidly that inasmuch as I had made the corner well enough it might perhaps be possible that my foot was not broken. He stared at me in the manner reserved for rebuking the insolent. He stared angrily at my right foot, which seemed to be supporting me. Although I had not committed the cardinal sin of contradicting my elders, it was plain that my foot had. He threw up his hands to Heaven and stalked off.

But there were many less spurious fractures. Catherine was the fastest runner among the girls. She ran with marvelous speed and grace and always won the prizes for foot-racing at the Fourth of July Field Day held down at Rutherford Field. As long as the sprints were outdoors, Catherine always finished intact. But when she ran in the gymnasium at Union School or Rutherford High School, she ran with an intensity that spurned any considerations of slowing down. Often, she slammed into the wall at the end of the gym. Too often, they helped her limp home.

Betty, athletic and aggressive, broke a collarbone in combat with the Prospect Place boys, while Elizabeth acquired a neatly split lip and a minor concussion during a back-yard duel in which the weapons were shovels at close quarters.

John was the unchallenged casualty champion. He continued to play football and baseball after he was graduated from high school, and continued to give it the old college try. He never slid into a base or ran at a line. He would dive at them. John was frequently carried home—once with a broken arm, and later with a broken collarbone. He also broke his leg, this time during a semi-pro football game. It was played during one of the periods of John's withdrawal from the despotism of the girls. Since he could not convalesce in his boarding-house room, he had to be taken home. Foddy glared his sympathy at him, and during the day, John was established in Foddy's big chair in the library, his crutches alongside him and his cast-encased leg propped up on a footstool.

At night, the Melrose A. C. boys trooped gaily into the house to comfort John and to scrawl mementos on the plaster. Those were the days of the popularity of the comic strip "Harold Teen," when fashionable young men and women wore yellow slickers covered with the bright sayings conned from that storehouse of wisdom. In India ink, you could read, "I love my wife, but, oh, you kid!" or "Nuts to you." or "It ain't no sin to take off your skin and dance around in your bones." These gems, together with girls' telephone numbers or drawings of curvaceous Betty Co-eds singing, "Boop-boop-a-doop," were inscribed by John's pals on his cast. When they had departed, Foddy would come downstairs from his room, where he had retreated, as he said, to save his sanity, and inspect the latest compositions of the Melrose bards. In silence, he would march up to John and look down at his leg.

"Lord!" he would say softly. "Let us admire universal education. Isn't it wonderful that so many of our young men have been taught how to read and write?"

Although I could not match John's success in achieving major breaks, I was passably adept at achieving small fractures and was perhaps his peer in cuts that needed stitching.

I broke my nose twice, each time while playing baseball and trying to stop a hot grounder. Such a misguided penchant for making the sterling play with my proboscis convinced me that I should be behind the plate, where I broke or dislocated a few of my fingers. But my nose was safely behind a mask. Not so my legs. Another boy, who had availed himself of his older brother's spiked shoes, and also, I suspect, his father's file, came flying into home plate and removed a square inch and a half of flesh below the calf of my right leg. How he managed to get at my right leg when it was my left side that was presented to him remains a riddle to me. I have always insisted that he ran around behind me and jumped—a claim which I might have advanced to forestall the accusation that I didn't know how to cover home plate. The hole was clamped together. It left a deep scar, a perfectly marvelous wound which, in later years, I displayed to Australian girls while regaling them with the fiction of having beaten off a Jap bayonet attack single-handed. In baseball, too, the bone above my left eye was laid open when a playful friend threw me a bat, forgetting to warn me that it was on its way.

In all of these mishaps, Foddy's displeasure was directed outward at the playmate involved. It was strange because it seemed to us almost instinctive with both him and Mother to hold their children culpable. No alibi, no explanation could ever deflect the flare-up that followed a bad report card from school or a brush with adult authority. Our teachers knew that they could depend on our parents' co-operation, and consequently we were kept busy intercepting letters from school and steaming them open, and in some cases forging excuses when one of us had played hookey. But when one of us got banged up, Foddy flew into a fury, damning "foreigners," if the playmates were not from the Western Islands, blasting the "bogtrotters," if they were.

I got banged up playing football, too. But apart from one minor concussion of the brain, it was nothing more serious than a few bruises or sprains or a rough tumble that might knock the wind out of me. This was perhaps odd, for I certainly played football more than the milder game of baseball, as did most of the boys in that football-loving town. The gridiron was the single passion of my boyhood. I played football in fair weather or foul, in daylight or darkness—and even an apparent eagerness to run errands for Mother could be traced to it.

A bottle of milk or a loaf of bread could be cradled

in the arm like a football, and the homeward dash from the A&P was like a glorious passage through a broken field, zigzagging through the trees as though they were tacklers, spinning away from a swamp maple here, straight-arming an oak there and finally bursting through the back door like old Seventy-Seven scoring standing up. After school I played pick-up games at Rutherford Field, and when the sky darkened, played myself home. It was a mile between the field and my house and the route was dotted with sand lots and scrub skirmishes. You could always get a game, and if the sides were even, you hurdled that impasse by agreeing to play safety for whichever team was on the defensive.

In those days, my pockets were stuffed with diagrams of football plays, most of them worked out during arithmetic classes, and my conversation was rich in the jargon of double reverses and Statue of Liberty plays. The finest Christmas present might be a biography of Knute Rockne. The most marvelous Christmas present of all was a pair of red football pants presented to me by a boy friend of Catherine's, an end on the professional Passaic Red Devils.

Doubtless, I wore them to bed, for I had them on when I awoke the next morning. In fact, they were not shucked throughout the entire Christmas holiday, until Foddy at last shouted in exasperation, "Has this boy no other clothes to wear?"

It seemed as if eighteen months, rather than seven, had

expired between New Year's and the arrival of autumn and the football season—and all of the time those gorgeous red pants, more glorious, now, with the white stripe I had painted down the back of each leg, lay at the foot of my bed like a promise of the grand days ahead.

You must understand that in those days a lad who appeared on the empty lots with so much as a helmet to wear was a well-equipped footballer indeed. If a boy had a pair of khaki football pants, his old man was rich. He might even be a sissy pretending that the uniform made the player. For a twelve-year-old to appear in red pants—red, mind you, when even the high school players had to content themselves with khaki, and not only this but also the very uniform of a professional—was to create a sensation. It was akin to the figure Patroclus must have cut when he stepped out of Achilles' tent wearing the boss' armor. And the results were almost as disastrous.

Tacklers exulted in slamming into those red pants with more than customary verve. Pilers-on took a savage glee in landing on the seat of the red pants while, in returning a punt or going out for a pass, the red one was a marked one. Worse, if the owner of the red pants appeared too big for his britches, the reverse of this was actually true. Just to run in them was challenge enough. They began somewhere beneath my armpits and ended somewhere below my ankles. Their weight was helpful in a goal-line plunge through these redoubtable ninety-pounders, but in a broken field, with one hand holding the ball and the other holding up the pants, the tactic of the straight-arm was denied me. But sometimes, clutched from behind by a last-ditch tackler, the runner in red could keep right on going, right out of the pants and over the goal line.

10

Betty and the
Unquiet Kiss

Dating, among the girls, was not a custom which Foddy could applaud. He opposed it for so long as he might, but once again, as in the matter of machinery, the times were such that he had to come to terms with it. The terms, of course, were Foddy's.

When the girls entered high school, and Mother advanced their cause, Foddy said that they might have dates. But first, the young man must present himself. He had "to meet Foddy." This was no facile confrontation. Many a star halfback on the high school football team must have yearned for the comparatively soft ordeal of an enemy tackler, rather than that short figure in reading robe and reading cap with the piercing eyes and formidable face. It was a mistake to park the car in front of our house and honk the horn. A long silence and the failure of any door to open would insinuate that perhaps it would be wise to go up the walk and ring the doorbell.

"Young man," Foddy would say, "this is not a roadhouse. If you wish to keep company with my daughter, please have the courtesy to show your face."

"Yes, sir," came the mumbled reply, and then, when the boy and the daughter had gotten out of earshot, there came an awed aside: "Boy, your old man looks just like the Pope."

Though they joked about "the Pope" behind his back,

they displayed a brisk and genuine respect in his presence, and they tried not to break his second rule, which was to get the girls home by ten o'clock. There was a third, but unexpressed rule, and perhaps Foddy considered this so obvious that it needed no articulation. No kissing.

On the night of Betty's first date, the rules were faithfully kept, except for the self-evident one, which was fractured. At ten o'clock, as Foddy sat reading in the library, there was the sound of the porch door opening, feet moving over the floor, voices, silence—and then, the sound of farewell, a good-night of the wet and smacking kind that the movies had made popular. It was—dare it be named?—a kiss.

The door flew inward and the startled couple gazed in alarm upon the Pope. And it was something of a papal anathema that rolled toward them.

"Young man, I will expect a written apology for this insult in the morning! Beatrice, go to your room!"

The youth gulped, nodded, and fled. Betty blinked and went softly up the stairs. In the morning, the apology was in the mailbox—delivered by hand. The following month provided Betty ample time in which to catch up on her homework.

Whenever the curfew was violated, Foddy rose from his chair, removed his cap and replaced it with his hat, seized the blackthorn stick that his father had brought from Ireland and issued out the door in search of what the family called "dirty stay-outs." His quarry might lead him to school gymnasiums where dances were being held, or to the homes of neighbors, but they were always flushed by a pounding on the front door, an angry question and a tapping of the stick. Then, one or another of the girls would come quietly forth.

Elizabeth was the most frequent object of Foddy's search, perhaps because she was the most daring and ingenious in slipping past the road blocks he erected along her path to glamour. She had the habit of attending high school basketball games in the afternoon and staying well past the end of the game for the more exciting soda with the fellows after it—and this while she was supposed to be home setting the table.

At half-past six, as the family dined, the door would open and Elizabeth's blond head would be poked cautiously into the room.

"Oh, gee, who set the table for me?"

"Elizabeth!"

"Yes, sir."

"Go to your room!"

As often as she was warned, she was delinquent, for she really liked basketball and sodas and fellows. The night of a dance, Elizabeth fell from grace again.

"You are not to go to that dance, do you hear me? You are not to go!"

She answered, "Yes, sir," and retreated to her room, not to beat her breast in repentance, but to devise some certain way of going to the dance. Her sisters rallied to her side. Catherine loaned her her best dress, Betty her coveted bunny jacket, Marion a pair of shoes, but no slip, Elizabeth, emphatically, no slip—and thus glamorously attired, she sat on her bed and waited for Madelon to report. Madelon had been stationed downstairs to spy on Foddy. The moment the book fell from his hands and his head sank forward on his chest, Madelon slipped out of the room and reported: "He's asleep, now."

"Okay," Catherine said, tying sheets together. "Get going, Elizabeth. And for goodness sake, don't tear my dress on your way down." Elizabeth nodded with a sincerity at odds with her reputation, and Catherine fastened one end of the tied sheets to the bed poster. The other end was dropped out the window.

Elizabeth slid down, waved a gay and grateful good-by, and disappeared in the dark in borrowed clothes and on feet that would soon be dancing.

An hour later, Foddy awoke.

"Marion," he said to Mother, "perhaps I was too harsh with that girl. Perhaps I'll let her go to the dance, after all." Mother nodded, for she never quarreled with clemency, and Foddy shouted, "Elizabeth, come down here."

Madelon appeared. "I think she went down to the store, Daddy." Foddy replied, "When she comes back, tell her I want to see her." Madelon retreated, consternated. All of the girls reflected sadly on the complications of life, how poor Elizabeth had broken jail just when she was about to be pardoned. Quietly, they scattered—to the laundry, to the attic, to the garage, to any place which might be safe from that explosive question now being raised repeatedly in the living room: "Where *is* that girl?" In a half hour or so, Foddy thought he might know the answer. He clapped on his hat, pulled the brim down all around, hefted his blackthorn stick and strode out the front door.

Down at St. Mary's gymnasium, Elizabeth glided dreamily in the arms of her escort—rapt. She hardly noticed a certain quiet creeping into the room. She paid no attention to the couples melting from the floor, ranging themselves in hushed awe on either side of the hall. Elizabeth thought that probably this number was a dancing contest and that she and her partner were winning. When the music stopped, and her escort also vanished, leaving the floor to her, and when she felt a tap upon her shoulder, Elizabeth thought happily that she, and she alone, had won. She turned, beaming.

"Come with me, Elizabeth!"

The blackthorn stick pointed an imperious exit, and Elizabeth bowed her head and followed it. But she lived, and it would be to defame the character of both Foddy and Elizabeth to suggest that this irrepressible head would be lowered long or that those impetuous feet would not soon be dancing again.

Foddy had his rules, but the girls had Mother. She sympathized with their reluctance to drag themselves away from a party just reaching its high point to hasten homeward before the grim stroke of deadline. Mother tempered Foddy's terms by leaving a key to the front door beneath a lamp on the porch and by devising a system of signals designed to get them safely past the Cerberus at the head of the stairs. She sat in the darkened sewing room in the front of the second story, waiting for a daughter to appear. When Mother turned the light on and off, this single wink meant: "Come ahead, he's asleep." If she turned it on and left it on, it warned: "Wait. He's still awake."

A more complicated code was developed to forfend against the ghastly chance of one of the girls being caught kissing. Mother believed that a little kissing never hurt anyone, a conviction which she confided to the girls, but kept from Foddy.

On nights when the girls came home in cars and the automobile doors did not immediately open, Mother resumed her sewing-room vigil. After five minutes, the lights upstairs winked furiously on and off, meaning: "That's enough!" If the door did not open and the daughter emerge, the hall lights blinked a peremptory message: "You're overdoing this!" In the event of failure here, the porch lights came brightly alight and stayed alight, glowering: "Get out of that car!" Finally, ignored on all three appeals, Mother came down the steps herself and yanked open the door to put her primitive means of communication into polished English: "Out of there, young lady, and into the house this minute!"

Inevitably, all of this dating produced a constant borrowing of clothes among the girls. Sometimes it was licit and sometimes illicit, and they had a saying among them that the first one out of the house was the best dressed.

It was not uncommon to hear a shriek of dismay. "My good dress! Who wore my good dress and left perspiration stains in it? For goodness sake, don't you ever take a bath, don't you ever use deodorant? Look at my good dress, it's ruined!"

More inevitably, it was the conscienceless Elizabeth who was most often the culprit. In her defense, it can be said that she was tempted. By the time Madelon and Elizabeth had entered the new parochial high school built by St. Mary's Parish, all of the older girls had passed through Rutherford High and had gotten secretarial jobs, which were regarded merely as the means of acquiring splendid wardrobes.

"Lord, Marion," Foddy would complain, "every penny these daughters of yours earn they spend on their backs."

So when Elizabeth reached high school, she resolved to distinguish herself as the best-dressed girl in her class. Academic distinction did not attract her, as it failed to enchant any of us. Our report cards always produced Foddy's unchanging lament: "Why do we bother, Marion? Must we go on forever, trying to make a silk purse out of a sow's ear?" Elizabeth was representative of this blithe defiance of instruction—like the rest of us, she was no stuffy bookworm.

She was fortunate in that most of the older girls' clothing fitted her, except for shoes, the tips of which could be stuffed with cotton, or lengthy hem lines, which could be swiftly pinned up to the proper height. But there was a difficulty. Marion, Catherine and Betty left for work later than Elizabeth left for school. Undaunted, Elizabeth chose to be late. Who would not suffer tardiness in the interests of style, who would balk at being a half hour late, if she could make her final appearance in splendor? For the sake of it, she was also willing to face the anger of her older sisters, when they would discover that an outfit ironed for use the next day had already been put into service by Elizabeth.

Betty acted. Her boy friend bought a lock and attached it to the door of her closet. Twenty-five cents got Elizabeth over this hurdle. She gave it to me to pick the lock.

These things always had a way of ending uproariously. One morning, Elizabeth waited until her sisters had gone and then availed herself of a freshly pressed dress of Marion's, a pair of her stockings and a pair of her shoes. She took up the hem, stuffed the shoes, and dressed. She walked across Carmita Avenue, already an hour late, but stylish. Down Carmita Avenue came a delivery truck, driven by a neighbor who conducted a tea-and-coffee business. Perhaps he was as intent upon admiring Elizabeth's clothes as she was. Whatever the reason, neither of them stopped and the truck made solid contact with Elizabeth.

To the neighbor's horror, she went down. To his dismay, she was up again in an instant, roaring at him in a tearful rage.

"My clothes! You've ruined Marion's clothes!"

"Are you hurt, dear?"

"Don't dearie me, you, you coffee man, you! Of course, I'm hurt. My dress is torn, the heels on my shoes are broken and my stockings are a mess. Hospital? What for? Just look at Marion's clothes! Oh, am I going to get it!"

With a shriek of despair, Elizabeth wheeled and ran into the house. She spent the remainder of the morning trying to repair the damage, but with no success. She spent the next month minding neighbors' children or raiding my cache of empty beer bottles trying to get the money to repay Marion. After that, she wore her own clothes to school, abandoning the goal of Best-Dressed Girl for some other triumph such as Most Popular or Best Personality or Girl with the Curliest Hair.

Both Elizabeth and Madelon were popular at school, as much for the hospitality of our house as for their own gay spirits. They had many parties. There was plenty of room for dancing, once the rugs were rolled back in the library and the front room. There was a piano and a record player, the ice box and pantry abounded in refreshments, and Foddy was known to have good liquor, although he had also the good sense to keep it hidden.

The night that St. Mary's High School's basketball team won the state championship in their group, it was decided to hold the victory celebration at our house. It was an on-the-spot decision, and before the happy victors trooped through the front door, Madelon was dispatched ahead of them to secure Foddy's permission for this impromptu party. He gave it and they entered. The party began.

Two of the young men went on a hunt for Foddy's liquor. They found it. They transferred it to the hall closet and returned to the party to spread the good news. For an hour or more the door to the front room kept opening and closing, as did the closet door, and the sounds of merrymaking rose steadily. Upstairs, Foddy lay in bed, listening.

"Marion, something's going on down there."

"Of course there is—they're enjoying themselves."

"Do you hear that commotion in the hall? What are they doing going to the closet so often?"

"Taking off their things, dear."

"What!" he bellowed, carrying the suggestion to an unintended conclusion, and he leaped out of bed. He put on his bathrobe and clapped on his cap and clattered downstairs. He went to the closet and flung the door open. Inside were two young men with tilted heads and Foddy's Scotch.

"Out!" Foddy bellowed. The sounds of merrymaking were stilled. The young men blinked and reached for their coats. Foddy leaned inside the closet, seized his blackthorn stick and retreated a step. He held the stick stiffly to his right, like an officer on parade with his sword, and pointed the way with his left. "Out!"

They left.

Then, the front room door flew open. The merrymakers gaped and shifted their feet uneasily.

"Out!"

They went. Though the account of the team's glorious victory on the basketball court was carried in all the local papers next morning, nothing was said about their utter defeat in our front hall. And the mortified Madelon and Elizabeth refused to go to school for two days until enough of their friends had telephoned them to assure them that Foddy's social crime had already taken on the outlines of a great joke.

Betty was the first to date seriously, just as she would later be the first to marry. But she and her fiancé had a terrible quarrel. He told her that he had had it and that as far as he was concerned it was all over. Betty was desolated. Sobbing, she told Elizabeth of her travail. But, suddenly, she grinned through the tears, and said, "I've got an idea."

"What?"

"I'm going down to the garage and read a magazine. You call him on the telephone and tell him I've run away from home. You know, I'm so broken up about it?"

Elizabeth did know. She knew one better. With a talent for improvement, she made the telephone call and said, "Have you seen Betty? No? Oh, I'm afraid she's going to do something terrible. We can't find her anywhere. Foddy found a note in her room saying that you two had broken up and that she doesn't want to live any more. Oh, yes, we've been to the river already. Oh, that's very sweet of you. Thank you. G'by."

While Betty sat in the car in the garage, chewing gum and leafing through a magazine, the distraught young suitor dashed madly about town, seeking his heart's love before she should pack it in. At last, weary and despondent, he came to the house and consulted Elizabeth.

"I've looked everywhere, but I can't find her."

"Did you try the garage?"

Perhaps Elizabeth did not intend that direful suggestion of carbon monoxide, but the look of fright upon the young man's face gave proof that it had occurred to him. He spun and dashed down Union Avenue to the garage. He found Betty, safe, smug and saucy. There had been no suicide, except, perhaps, that which he had visited upon his own resolve.

11

Mother's Clocks
Went Cuckoo

Even with Mother's signals and that blessed key beneath the porch lamp, late-returning daters and common stay-outs had always a last terrifying obstacle to surmount before getting safely into bed: the front stairs. These stood in the hall, running up to the second floor, where most of the bedrooms were. Justly feared, they were justly famed as well.

Many marvelous scenes were enacted in the front hall, in full view of anyone crouching on the stairs. Madelon and I sat there often at night, when we should have been in bed, waiting for something to happen or for the door-bell to ring and someone to enter, or else just listening to the serious, grown-up voices rising and falling in the two front rooms.

From the stairhead, Madelon and I played a game called "Cut the cable." Betty had taken us to the Rivoli to see Douglas Fairbanks dueling and leaping about in a typical Fairbanksian melodrama. In one scene, the acrobatic Fairbanks stands on the quarter-deck of a ship, driving off a pack of boarders with his flashing sword. As he fights, the skipper shouts, "Cut the cable, cut the cable," meaning, sever the boarders' grappling line. Douglas does it, in a single, glittering stroke—and the vessel floats free.

The moment we had returned home, Madelon dashed

upstairs for a blanket and I darted to the kitchen for string and a pair of bread knives. We fastened the blanket to two rungs. By turns, we cried, "Cut the cable!" and hacked at the string with our knives—shouting in glee when it dropped in a wonderful enshrouding surprise upon young men standing in the hall below.

It was a joy to behold the reactions of those visitors. When that ghoulish shriek burst out above their heads, looking up, they saw the flash of steel and, plummeting down, a dark misshapen mass that could have been a body or a huge bird. They shouted or tried to duck, or, caught, struggled frantically in the folds of the unknown thing that suffocated them.

Marion and Catherine considered cutting the cable the pastime of ill-bred brats. When it happened, and the caller was caught, they assisted him to freedom with a weak smile. "Oh, that's just our little sister and brother. Won't you come in and meet Foddy?" While this second ordeal was being sustained, another of the older girls would be detached from the main body to come galloping up the stairs in a punitive foray designed to chastise the stairhead guerrillas.

Of course, cutting the cable ended in total annihilation of the irregulars one night. Too hastily, we sighted our victim. Too hastily, the cry rang out and the knives swung. Too hastily, the blanket fell on Foddy. It was the end.

There were other interesting scenes to be watched from the stairhead. Once, the doorbell rang and Foddy answered it. The caller was a policeman.

"I've come to pick up your driver's license, Mr. Leckie. Orders of the judge."

"Judge! Who do you think you are addressing, officer?"

The policeman blinked uncomfortably. "John J. Leckie. Convicted of reckless driving."

The policeman drew back a step before that rising bellow of anguish. "Marion, what has that son of yours done, now? How many times must I tell that boy to sign his name Junior?" The police officer was forcefully informed that Foddy had no license, that he did not drive, that he despised automobiles and every other triumph of industrial progress, that the culprit was undoubtedly his oldest son who, of course, was modern enough to know how to drive, though not old-fashioned enough to know how to sign his name, and that if the officer were not as yet married he would be wise indeed to remain in that unharassed state.

The next day, the news of John's brush with the traffic laws was in the local paper, and, of course, the identifying "Junior" did not follow his name. This was one of the occasions when John packed up again, and Foddy took to walking to the station to avoid the gibes of commuters who had read the paper. "Blasted extroverts," he muttered. "Ha, ha, ha—just like it is in the funny papers."

In later years, a similar piece of intelligence was printed in the local paper, although on this occasion it was my name that graced the front page: "LECKIE YOUTH ARRESTED FOR SPEEDING." Though I had already taken the precaution of burning the copy delivered to our house, those jolly commuters had advised Foddy of the newest notoriety of his household. In fact, it wasn't I who had done the speeding. It was a friend, who had eluded the Rutherford cops in a mad, eighty-mile-an-hour dash to a party in Passaic. I was there and drove home with him. He asked me to drive, pointing out that he had no driver's license and that if the police recognized the car, they would arrest me by mistake. Then, he said, with Hibernian persuasiveness, I could prove that it hadn't been me. Well, they did stop the car and they did arrest me, but they didn't bother much about my attempts to prove my innocence. They booked me. The paper came out next day, and there I was, on the front page, and there, as I stood at the head of the stairs, was Foddy in the hall below, brandishing the newspaper and dancing with fury.

"Marion! Oh, Lord, where is that woman? Marion, come here and read the latest episode in the saga of the Leckie family!"

I holed up in the attic until the thunderbolts had ceased to ricochet off the walls, until the lightning had stopped crackling, until Elizabeth stole softly up the stairs, and said, "You can come down, now. He's eaten his dinner."

I confronted him and told all. He regarded me with a mixture of wonder and disbelief.

"And now you are a noble friend, Robert—a martyr, perhaps? Now you are playing Damon to this"—a dreadful, inward-breathing struggle—"this young hooligan's Pythias?"

I had better sense than to agree.

"Or do you think that actually you are only a sucker, Robert?"

There—there, now, was an assessment which I could be expected to share.

"Yes, sir."

His eyes rolled and he roared, "Get your mendacious friend on the telephone, Robert, and tell him I want to speak to his father."

I obeyed. Foddy spoke to the friend's father in a brief dictatorial conversation which ended: "And now you will take your son down to the police station and acquaint them with the truth." And that was what happened.

But the front stairs, though they offered a vantage from which to view the episodes of the family saga unfolding, were also to be feared because they creaked. No matter how stealthily they were ascended, they protested in dry, cracking moans. Foddy slept lightly and a single loud creak sent him springing from his bed in his room at the head of the stairs. He bounded out the door with a flashlight winking in his hands. Next to cap, hat and stick he was distinguished by that torch. He used it to look for books, to make bed checks and to inspect the gas stove and the door and window locks.

You would be impaled in its light, like an airplane in a searchlight beam, while Foddy demanded, "Who is there?" No reply was expected, for he had seen, and the torch had swept over to the clock on the hall bookcase. "Twelve o'clock, eh? Well, your mother will find plenty of things to keep you home for the next few days. Go to bed!"

Foddy might also swing his nose in an arc close up to the mouth of the challenged one, sniffing suspiciously for an aroma of alcohol beneath the scent of spearmint.

Mounting the stairs tried our ingenuity. Betty's method was to slip out of her shoes in the hall, tie them together and loop them around her neck. Then, on light, stockinged feet, keeping to the firmer inside portion of the steps, she ran the gantlet. Typically bold, Elizabeth shunned the stairs. She left her pajamas and blankets on the porch before she went out. Returning, she undressed and slept on the porch studio couch until dawn, when she would slip in and go nonchalantly up the stairs as though she had just gone down them in her bedclothes for a glass of orange juice. It worked, and it didn't work. Bed checks defeated her.

Madelon, of course, had the superior style. But this was owing more to her standing than to her skill. When

Foddy confronted her with flashlight and inquiring nose, Madelon merely snorted, "Oh, pooh to you!" and walked past him to her room.

My own method owed something to Betty's and something to myself. With my shoes around my neck, I lay flat on the banister and pulled myself up, rung by painful rung. It required strength and steady nerve, but it did work.

Catherine was the cleverest. She hit upon a scheme that was stunning in its simplicity. Before she left the house, she turned all of the clocks back two hours. She had the daring and foresight to enter Foddy's room and do the same to the pocketwatch on his bureau.

But Catherine had to get up early in the morning to restore the stolen two hours to all of the clocks in the house, and this soon took its toll.

There were many clocks in the house, all jealously tended by Mother. She wound them regularly with loving care and fidelity, moving from room to room with a bunch of keys jangling on a string. Owing to the untimely death of a number of the less hardy clocks unable to endure Catherine's disturbing fingers, there were more keys than clocks. You could hear Mother fumbling with her keys, mumbling, "Pshaw! Where *is* the right key?" The strange behavior of the clocks, the sight of so many of them languishing, moved Mother to compassion. She tried to resurrect them, giving them new life by taking them apart and reincarnating them with alien organs.

Thus saved, the clocks became exuberant in their gratitude, and this came to our rescue as we climbed the treacherous stairs.

The clocks competed with one another in striking astronomical hours such as thirty-eight o'clock or half-past forty-five, and beneath these clamorous contests you could slip unheard past Foddy's door. If the clock in the front hall rang a gentle, mellow eighteen, the upstairs hall clock answered with a harsh and metallic twenty— while from the sewing room the old walrus of Mother's brood boomed back at them with twenty-four, twenty-seven, and so on up to the thirties, until the others had been beaten into terrified silence, leaving this grizzled old campaigner alone in the field, booming on and on like a triumphant warrior still slashing the air with strokes above the fallen foe. Occasionally, the dainty, glass-enclosed French clock on the library mantel timidly sought to join the fun, but its tinkling was as the plaintive plucking of a pizzicato against the baying brass upstairs.

At times, they awoke Foddy and we could hear him hiss to Mother, "Listen, Marion, those clocks of yours have gone cuckoo."

"I can't understand it," she would reply, bewildered. "I can't understand what's gotten into them."

12

"Put St. Joseph out the Window!"

Since we were a Catholic family, our religion was part of the air we breathed. All of us had spent at least a few years in parochial school, most of us more than that, and the three youngest—Elizabeth, Madelon and I—went on to parochial high school. We knew our catechism and our Bible history and we received the Sacraments. There was a large, plaster crucifix at the head of the stairs and a lovely, oval-framed print of a Renaissance painter's Madonna and Child in the library. Holy pictures adorned the walls of all the bedrooms, and in Elizabeth and Madelon's room there was a little shrine to the Virgin and St. Joseph.

But these were the forms, and we were not a formal family. The Faith did not end with pictures or statues, forgetting the meaning or presence behind them. It was not a sterile thing, suffocated in formulae or bound up merely with dutiful attendance at Sunday Mass or listening to speeches at Communion breakfasts. It was a way of life, touching on all of our life, and it was constantly being interpreted for us by Foddy or Uncle Tom.

Uncle Tom was the dining-room theologian. He would be asked by the girls to decide if it were a venial or a mortal sin for their brother to have stolen their fudge, or for any of them to have borrowed Mother's charge-a-plate to obtain a new pair of shoes at Hahne's department store in Newark. But we never took him too seriously in these matters, except, of course, if there was actually some point of doctrine to be mastered for religion classes at school.

Foddy encouraged discussion of religion at the dining table. But religious sham could bring down a scathing rebuke. Should one of us simper over a plaster saint seemingly born holy, to die after a life as sweet and dainty as the figure of a bride on a wedding cake, Foddy would roar his disapproval. "Saints! Fanatics, you mean. Who could live with them?"

Then, seeing us startled, sensing that he had us, he would rush on to explain that if a saint was anything he was not sweet. He was tough. We would hear of St. Ignatius standing up to his neck in a frozen pond or of the Irish monks living on nettle soup. We would learn that some great saints had first been great sinners. St. Francis, Foddy's favorite, had taken money from his father to rebuild an abandoned church. The lovable friend of birds and beasts had suffered the stigmata and once offered to jump into a fire to prove a point to the Sultan. Saints, we would hear, were the only real successes, living proof of the validity of Christianity. They were ordinary human beings who had been touched with the fire of the love of God, and this, he would explain, was why the world quite justly regarded them as fanatics and why we could not live with them.

"Because they wouldn't leave you alone."

"Put St. Joseph out the Window"

If we were in church, and a person moved down the aisle with exaggerated reverence in gait and downcast eyes, he would nudge Madelon and say, "See that holy joe? His shoes are too tight." Officious ushers irritated him, especially those who sought to cram another worshipper into a place already occupied by Foddy's ample bulk.

Though Foddy practiced and lived by the Faith, and had been a lay catechist as a young man, he abstained from church social activity. Parish suppers were not for him or his. He gave generously to the church, but avoided bazaars and bingo games.

Foddy was scornful of people who, in his phrase, canonized their own opinions. He was eager to show us where the Faith was strong—in its Sacraments and its teaching and its power to guide life, and where it was weakened by people who confused custom or discipline for articles of faith. He wanted our faith to be strong enough for our minds to be free and active in it.

So it was not a cold gray thing for us, but alive and to be lived, and since humor accounted for a good part of the living in our house, we often made jokes about it.

If we were at dinner and grace was being said, and Catherine had jumped the gun, Foddy would frown and say, "Bless us, O Lord, for these Thy gifts which we are about to receive—and for those which Catherine has already received—through Thy bounty through Christ our Lord, amen."

153

Elizabeth was a great fan of St. Anthony's, the saint who is the patron of the lost-and-found departments. This was because Elizabeth was forever losing things, and forever sinking to her knees to beseech St. Anthony to find them for her. When she prayed to St. Anthony and looked for them, she often found them. When she merely prayed, she did not—and she would be a bit resentful that the scheduled miracle had not come off. It never occurred to Elizabeth that her prayer had been answered, that the reply might have been "No," or "Not until you start looking yourself." Elizabeth never swerved from her faith in the efficacy of prayer in material as well as spiritual matters. She would make novenas in the interests of a bid to the Junior Prom as well as the strength to resist the temptation of her sisters' clothing. Nor did she abandon the practice in later years, when her own children began to appear and the novenas became petitions to move stubborn bowels or to improve failing marks.

Poor St. Joseph. His little statue was never left alone, for both Elizabeth and Madelon kept putting him out the window to banish gray skies or to stop the rain. The moment a downpour began, the cry would be raised, "Hey, Madge—hurry up and put St. Joseph out the window."

Often, when Madelon was going swimming on a Saturday afternoon with her girl friends, many of whom were Protestants, the telephone would ring.

"Madge?"

"Yes?"

"Is St. Joseph out the window?"

"No. Why?"

"It looks like rain. You'd better hurry up and put him out."

Down would go the telephone and up the stairs would go Madelon and out the window would go the patron saint of families—the friend of fair weather in the service of Protestants and Catholics alike.

Superstition?

Never! Ask Madelon, ask her friends, ask Foddy, ask me. All will vow that it never rained on those Saturdays. Nor did St. Joseph ever, as that gloomy atheist fellow is now suggesting, get wet.

Religion, with its forms, was so much a part of our being that we often gave unconscious expression to it. Sometimes ludicrously. The girls shouted with laughter the time Elizabeth and I returned from the Rex—a flea-bitten theater in East Rutherford which Foddy called "the bucket of blood."

"Know what he did?" Elizabeth said, pointing to me. "The picture was on when we got inside. It was dark. When we got to our seat, he genuflected and blessed himself! He would have knelt down, too, if I hadn't knocked him into his seat."

Sometimes Mother and Foddy would begin to argue

in their room upstairs. Their voices could be heard, and then, suddenly, only Mother's—carrying on a lonely diatribe, indicting this, accusing that, blaming and challenging before ending with a withering taunt. Silence. Incredible defeat. Then, Mother's voice again: "Well, what do you have to say about that?" More silence, and Mother's voice rising in irritation, "Answer that one, if you can. Say something! Oh, why don't you say something?"

"BECAUSE I'M SAYING MY PRAYERS!"

Religion carried over to those moments of sadness, such as when one of the cats had died. There would be a burial service in the back yard. A grave would be dug, the poor stiff little body would be lowered into it, and someone would read a passage from the Sunday missal over it. A cross would be made of sticks and stuck at the head of the tiny grave, and we would leave the funeral confident that we would meet these departed friends in Heaven—especially Lindy the Second, an eccentric who was well-remembered for his hatred of whistling and his fondness for dishrags.

There was religion in fish-on-Friday, which everyone but Mother and Foddy detested, preferring, if we could get someone to make it, an omelette or potato pancakes or a Welsh rarebit. If a Holy Day or National Holiday fell on Friday and the diocese was dispensed from abstinence, what joy to arise on Friday morning savoring the prospect of bacon for breakfast, to be topped at lunch by ham sandwiches and perhaps steak-and-onions for dinner. On these days, we knew well the virtue of obedience. If the bishop said you could eat meat, well, do what the bishop says and eat it. Conversely, the day after Thanksgiving was always one of unrequited hunger. We had to contemplate the unfinished turkey aware that we could not touch it, and that by the next day, Saturday, it would be too dry to taste. Now, there is penance!

Religion could be at the bottom of a minor economic crisis. Mother and Foddy debated frequently over where Mother's money had gone. As it happens in the best of families, Mother said she never had enough money and Foddy said he would welcome a hard, dollars-and-cents definition of that desired state.

"It is quite obvious, Marion," he would say, reaching for his pocketbook or calling for his checkbook, "that by 'enough' you merely mean, 'more.'"

Once, after a normal mid-week exchange of this sort, Foddy said to me, "Robert, does your mother gamble?"

I was astonished. "Do you mean play bridge with the Moms' A. C.?"

"No. I mean gamble. Robert, have you ever heard your mother say anything about horses?"

I shook my head, grinning, and he clapped his, grimacing.

"I can't understand it. Where does her money go?"

At that moment, there was granted to me an insight,

an answer to his question. "Here," I said, pointing to the pile of letters and little magazines on Mother's desk. They were from missionaries all over the world. "Did you ever think of this?"

He picked some of them up and riffled through them. He seemed puzzled at first, but then his eyes rolled in dismay and his jowls began to droop in defeat.

"Listen, Robert," he said softly. "Listen to this. In China, you can save a child for five dollars. There's a Franciscan who has a mission in the South who will remember you in his prayers for two. . . . Ah, here's a modest fellow. Only a quarter needed for his Indian lads in South Dakota. *He* won't last. Not with this kind of competition. Though I must say that I'll miss him." He put the letters down and picked up the magazines. I noticed that he was reading only the inside covers, where the subscription price was printed, and I could see that he was doing mental arithmetic. He placed them on the desk.

"Well," he said, sighing, "now I know." He turned to leave the room.

"What are you going to do?" I asked.

"I might appeal to the Papal Curia," he replied, "but I have reason to doubt the impartiality of that body in a case of this character. I am going to do nothing. As your mother would say, Robert, this is just another cross that I must bear."

If Foddy made no appeal to ecclesiastical authority regarding Mother's disposition of the house money, one of her cleaning women did. And when she did, she skipped the customary, temporal channels and went straight to headquarters. Mother always had difficulty with cleaning women. If the woman happened to be busy downstairs, Mother would find something upstairs for her to do. If she began to iron, Mother would think that it was a good day for washing. Added to this harrying interference was a sort of charitable badgering which would require the woman to drop everything and come to the breakfast nook for a cup of tea. But when the day was done and all of the work was not, Mother became unjustly annoyed. Once she got into an argument with a cleaning woman. She accused her of loafing and said that she was going to dock her pay a dollar. It was, of course, only a threat, but the woman took it for truth. Shrieking aloud, she dashed into the library to throw herself on her knees before the Madonna and Child.

She burst into infuriated, voluble entreaty—shaking her fist at the Virgin, pointing angrily at Mother and calling upon the Holy Family to punish the author of this injustice. Mother stood in the doorway with her arms folded. "Humph!" she snorted. "A fine way to act in front of Our Lady."

Goaded by this, the woman shrieked again and beat her breast in anguish, and Mother replied, "Go ahead, she isn't listening." At this point, Foddy came home from work and into the library. He stopped, aghast. He rushed to the woman's side and helped her to her feet. She transferred her fire to him. He blanched, pulled a wad of bills from his pocket and pressed the just wage into the woman's hands, plus an extra dollar for heart balm. The woman's mouth snapped shut and she marched from the room without pausing to thank the Virgin for this rapid intercession on her behalf.

Foddy wheeled on Mother. "Marion," he said, "have you ever read St. Paul's letter to the Corinthians?"

"Humph!" she snorted, and Foddy quoted: "'. . . these three abide, Faith, Hope and Charity, but the greatest of these is Charity.'"

"Grandstander!" Mother jeered, and returned to the kitchen.

Knowledge of the New Testament was one of Foddy's means of keeping us on the straight and narrow path of our religion. If one of us was suspected of having missed Mass, Foddy met the suspect at the door with the question, "Did you attend Mass this morning?"

"Yes, sir."

"Splendid. Give me a precis of the gospel read at the Mass this morning."

If this test could not be passed, it would do no good to say, either in truth or falsehood, that you had not been listening when the priest read the gospel. If you had been at Mass, you were supposed to have been present in mind as well as body. Not to know the gospel was proof that you had not been completely there. No excuse was possible, and one result of this was that all of us learned the New Testament fairly well.

Only once was Foddy outwitted at these after-Mass confrontations. Madelon and I had been to confession the night before and somehow, probably because we had broken our fast, we did not receive Communion next day. When I reached home I found Foddy waiting for me in a quivering rage.

"What do you mean by committing a mortal sin, refusing to receive Communion?"

"Excuse me, sir, but that's not a mortal sin. It's what is called rejecting grace."

He glared, for a moment undecided. Then he whirled and dashed into the living room, where I could hear him consulting Uncle Tom. When the door opened again, and Madelon stepped in, he bounded toward her fiercely. "What do you mean by rejecting grace that way, young lady?"

It was a triumph—solitary, not to be repeated—but still a triumph.

13

Footprints on the Porch Roof

Mysteries in our house were of two classes, major and minor. Quite naturally, there were more of the lesser puzzles, and these were usually recurrent—mystifying not so much in how they began but in how they would end. Betty's sleepwalking was of this character.

When Betty arose from her cot in the sleeping porch to drift somnolently through the halls, a giggling, night-gowned wraith, the question we asked ourselves was whether Betty was going swimming or going to church. The answer came in the morning.

If Betty was discovered in the bathtub, it would be clear that she had left her bed for a midnight dip. If she was found crouched in a kneeling position within the wicker laundry hamper at the foot of the attic stairs in the sewing room, it could be deduced that she had answered a call to worship. The hamper was Betty's church. As often as Mother confronted her there and ordered her out and back to bed, Betty replied in an outraged whisper, "Shh! I'm in church. No talking in church, Mother."

Though exasperated, Mother feared to shake her, because she had read or heard somewhere that somnambulists were to be treated gently and not to be shocked while sleepwalking, lest it damage their minds. So Mother sat by with impatient patience, waiting for the dawn that would pronounce an *ite, missa est* in Betty's church.

Another recurrent mystery was The Case of the Damp Toilet Seat. But this was soon solved by the girls, and Marion thought to put a stop to it by hanging a sign in the bathroom, which proclaimed: "Please lift the lid —we're sick of getting wet heinies!"

It was intended for me, but it was read by Foddy. There was a howl of outraged propriety, the sound of ripping cardboard and then a sharp bang, signifying that the lid was being lowered by the master of the house.

The mystery of what had happened to Foddy's cuff links was unraveled when Elizabeth appeared in a new pair of shoes, purchased with what they had brought at the Old Gold shop downtown; while the Case of Foddy's Missing Cigars might have been solved by a visit to the West End Firehouse, where the volunteers puffed gladly on Havanas purchased at the bargain rates of two for a nickel.

Most of us could guess who had taken the car out last night without permission and used up all the gas, whose empty applejack bottles were heaped against the woodpile outside our summer house at the lake, who had been wearing Catherine's best shoes, or who was helping himself to Foddy's ties, what broad-beamed boy friend had broken the sofa in the front room, or which thirsty caller had drained a bottle of rum and sought to conceal the theft by refilling it with black coffee, what was the significance of the deliberately broken lock on the dining-room window (to assist late home-comers), who made fudge in the kitchen and left the dirty pans in the sink, what cheat had marked every deck of cards in the house as a precaution against defeat in penny poker or bridge, who took a bath last and left a ring around the tub, or what was the name of the finicky greedy-guts who squeezed all the chocolates in the Christmas candy boxes to get at all the best cream centers, who kept using the big dictionary to stand on to reach Mother's penny hoard in the larcenous delusion that Indian-heads were worth two cents, who let the fire go out, who forgot to sweep the porch, rake the leaves, shovel the sidewalk, let out the cat, bring in the dog, empty the garbage, close the door—who was smoking in bed (everybody!) and which vulgar girl was using Foddy's razor blades to shave her legs (all of them).

These were lesser mysteries, and they were perhaps mysterious only to Foddy. They could not come up to the excitement or round-eyed wonder that was produced on the morning that Foddy discovered the footprints in the snow on the porch roof.

Here was a puzzler, here was a case, here was a mystery most inexplicable, most mystifying and most major.

"Burglars!" Foddy shouted, the moment he had gotten out of bed and looked out his window to see Rutherford blanketed in snow. "Marion, come here and look! We've been burgled."

Not only Mother but all of us came dashing to his window, and Foddy was so excited he omitted to censure us for having entered without knocking. We saw a line of deep footprints, moving away from Foddy's window in the direction of the sewing room. We scampered into the sewing room. The prints ran past the window toward the roof edge on the right. Foddy strained and heaved the window up, cursing its balkiness, as usual.

"Look, Marion, they run all the way to the edge of the roof!"

They did. The prints began at Foddy's bedroom window, almost at the left edge of the roof, and moved with neat, sunken precision across the snow to the farther, or right, edge. We looked at him. Had he been walking in his sleep? If so, had he put on his shoes first? But how did he get back? Maybe he jumped!

As though uniformly struck with this grand idea, all of us whirled and dashed down to the porch, still clad in pajamas. But, no, there was not a single depression in that smooth, soft expanse of whiteness. We trooped back upstairs, disappointed. Foddy was on the edge of his bed, in his bathrobe, now, and his eyes narrowed in thought, his chin outthrust in indignant bewilderment. He spoke.

"Where is Thomas?"

"Still up in bed," someone answered.

"Call him," he began, but then, changing his mind, he grunted and stalked past us and climbed the attic stairs himself. We heard voices, one demanding, the other denying, the first scoffing, the second snickering—and then a muffled snort, followed by the sound of Foddy marching down the stairs, with a pair of Uncle Tom's shoes in his hand. He leaned out the open window and fitted a shoe into the print. It rattled around in it. He snorted and pulled back. He went into John's room and returned with a pair of his shoes. Again the experiment, again the failure to fit. He even tried his own, but they were far too small. At an order, we rounded up all the galoshes in the house. All of them were tried, none fit. Quite obviously, Foddy had abandoned the notion of burglary and now suspected Uncle Tom or John of a tipsy, late-evening, breath-of-air-catching stroll on the roof. But, beyond the fact that not a shoe in the house would fill those prints, he was defeated by their singular direction and their abrupt end.

The police were called. They came, looked, scratched their heads, made inquiries about sleepwalkers, and finally agreed that the worst thing about it was that you just couldn't figure it out. Somebody suggested that the porch-walker might have leaped from the roof edge to a tree in our neighbor's yard—but it was decided that the tree was too far away. The police left. The mystery remained.

Thrilled and delighted, we ate breakfast and hastened to school, bursting to brag of the mysterious footprints on our porch roof. At noon time, and after school, each of us brought home a friend or two to display the proof. The stairs and the hallway became wet and muddied from dripping boots, until Mother, driven beyond patience, ordered everybody out.

Foddy came home from work early and immediately bounded up the stairs to the sewing room. He ate his dinner in thoughtful silence, before returning to his vigil. For two nights, he sat up late in the darkened sewing room, his blackthorn stick beside him and a flashlight in his hand.

On the morning of the third day, we were awakened to the sound of strenuous puffing and scraping noises on the roof. Foddy was shoveling the mystery into oblivion. He stood out there, in a bathrobe and cap, heedless of commuters gathered gaping on the corner, and thrust those irritating footprints out of his sight. We were astonished, not only to see him on the roof, but to contemplate him with a snow shovel in his hands.

This was unique, a departure from habit alone sufficient to perpetuate the mystery.

In a less amusing way, there was also for us, as for all other growing children in cold or temperate climates, the overpowering mystery of winter. Perhaps I should have said winter snow, for this is what I mean—the soft, mysterious whiteness of it, drifting down from on high, seeming to materialize from only thirty feet or so above your head, as though descending from an unseen cause

like the little salt mill at the bottom of the ocean that
keeps turning and turning in the legend of why the sea is
salty. How children love snow, opening their mouths
even to let the flakes fall and melt upon their tongues,
watching anxiously to see that it does not stop, satisfied
only when it begins to mount in soft mounds, covering
the ugly winter grass, softening the starkness of the bare
trees, curving the street corners and stretching a blanket
over front terraces and back yards, whitening the black
roofs and making the very air hushed and pregnant with
a promise of snowball fights and sledding. Then there is
the almost unbearable happiness if it should start to snow
on Christmas Eve.

Snow meant all of this to us, even the pang of disappointment when it stopped, for there is no snowfall,
however deep, that can fully content a child. We did the
usual things, built snow men in the yard or piled up
snow forts for snowball fights. We went sledding, too—
at first in the back yard, where there was a three-foot
terrace, unbelievably and dangerously high. But we
risked it, sometimes with one of the cats, Snoopy, or one
of the innumerable Lindys who lived and died with us,
riding as reluctant passengers. If we piled up at the foot
of the garden, the cat would wriggle free and scamper
away in anger, stepping daintily in the snow and shaking
each paw with the petulant hostility which cats seem
to reserve especially for snow. Often, the sledding ended
in a quarrel and a flood of tears, when Elizabeth, tiring

of this tame sport with the young ones, deliberately tripped us up or pelted us with snowballs, hoping to drive us indoors with complaints to Mother so that she might slip off to Washington Avenue where the big kids were sledding. Elizabeth had no fondness for sticking around the house and no love for the chore of minding the little ones, though she had a passion for mixing with others, especially for running errands for neighbors. With succinct scorn, Mother tagged this infuriating characteristic in a phrase that should stand forever: "Street angel, house devil."

When Madelon and I were older, at ten years or more, we also went sledding on Washington Avenue. Although sledding was good during the day, it was splendid at night. Enough sleds had sped down the slope to pack the snow, the cold of evening had hardened it— and to this was added the romance of the night, the dark figures gathered at the crest of the hill, where a wooden horse had been placed to prevent autos from entering. Red lanterns were suspended from it. In the light of these, the street lamps overhead and the pale yellow beams lancing out from the windows of the houses, the gay sledders assembled in their lumpy winter clothing, shouting to one another, challenging each other to races, and the girls shrieking with feigned anger when the big boys coasted up behind them to grasp the rear of their sled and overturn it or send it veering into a snow bank.

This was called "tripping"—and the most daring trippers were the objects of more admiration than were the lads with fastest sleds.

Should the snow begin to fall as you sledded, the seeming silence of it heightened the other noises you heard on the hill, the slam of sleds being thrown down, the thump of the body leaping on it, the hiss of runners against the snow, the shrill cries of the girls and the hoarse guffawing of the boys, and all around this oasis of merriment, the clanking *cap-thock, cap-thock* of autos rolling over the streets on skid-chains.

We continued to sled until our clothes were stiff and crusted with snow, until our lips were blue and our teeth chattering, until our hands were numb in their board-like mittens, and then we ran home, to drape our clothes, dripping, on the radiator, and go into the kitchen for a cup of hot chocolate.

On the Washington Avenue hill, there was always a dare that no one took. The saying was that if you stuck your tongue out on the cold sled runners, it would stick to it. Always, some boy was taunting a girl, hoping to inveigle her into it, eager to see if it was true. I never saw the challenge accepted, but, like the others, I insisted that I had done it and had to carry tongue-and-sled gingerly home to thaw it free.

It was on the hill that I encountered, and was routed by, sex. Until I was twelve or thereabouts, the war against women had been total. The feminine gender might as well have been neuter, for all it meant to me as gender. God had seen fit to make creatures with high voices, long hair and wide hips—creatures so awkwardly devised that they could neither catch nor throw a baseball or return a punt, so slow afoot that they could be overtaken by the most lumbering policemen, so silly that they giggled when they should have been grave and wept when they should have laughed—strange, soft beings fond of bathing salts and clean clothes. But it was not their fault that they had been so made. They were to be pitied—but from a distance.

Some of my friends on the hill were narrowing this distance, going to Capua, as the saying goes. Even the boldest "trippers" occasionally surrendered, and they could be seen sneaking a bellywhopper down the slope with a giggling girl sprawled atop them. It was a sad sight. Outwardly, I showed my contempt, but inwardly I began to wonder if there was not something to it. At last, a girl suggested that I give her a ride. I looked around to see if any of my sisters was present. No power on earth could bring me to go sledding with a girl before the scornful eyes of the girls. It would have meant to them that after six or seven years of warfare their natural enemy had meekly spiked his guns, hauled down his flag and thrown up his hands—betraying the postern of the fortress where Foddy, Uncle Tom, and John slept on, trusting that the foe was still without the walls. I looked around and saw none of them and said, "Okay."

I threw down my sled, congratulating myself that this

girl, at least, was a known tomboy, and that if it came to exposure my defection was still defensible. I threw it down and sprawled flat and the girl flung herself on top of me—and the walls came tumbling down.

So this was what brought all those he-man football players to our house! So this was what had tripped up the daring trippers. How wise, Ulysses, to bind yourself and stuff your seamen's ears with wax. How long, how long, O Lord, has this been going on? I raced home, pulling my sled after me, warmly confused, delightfully disconcerted and wondering if it were not getting to be time to talk of armistice.

14

River, You
Go Your Way

One of the things that distinguished our family at Lake Erskine was our possession of a cocker spaniel who hated water. Bojangles could not swim. He refused to swim. He was absolutely unashamed of this defect, which, in a breed of water dog, was a clear contradiction in terms. He did not like, even, to ride on water—and on the few occasions on which Bojangles could be coaxed or bullied into the canoe, he would stand awkwardly in the bow, his legs stretched stiffly outwards, his black ears drooping despondently and his nose quivering apprehensively, as though he were sniffing the air for a scent of the dear old earth that he had left behind him. The moment the craft touched land, Bojangles was gone with a yelp of relief and a wild sprint for the safety and solidity of the woods.

I had just turned fourteen when Bojangles came to stay with us. He was our first dog. Though we had always had at least one cat, we had not been able to persuade Foddy to let us have a dog. But a business friend of his, perhaps unaware of this prohibition, presented Bojangles to us. He rang the front doorbell one day in early spring, and when I opened the porch door, he deposited a black bundle of fur in my hands. He was named Bojangles a few moments later and he thumped his tail in pleasure. But when he was given his first bath, he snarled with all the ferocity of a ten-week-old puppy. His pedigree might describe him as having been trained to water, but Bojangles was an emphatically un-dogmatic dog. He was a heretic. He would go to the stake before he went to the spout. He remained in the water-filled laundry tub for the space of that measure of time which permitted him to get his legs under him to spring out again. His eyes rolled and he yelped and yelped while dashing about the laundry, rolling on the floor, upsetting the laundry basket, sprawling over the spilled wash and finally scampering into the furnace room to scramble to the top of the coal pile where he crouched in palpitating fear—only the terrified whites of his eyes marking him out against that ebony background.

Bojangles had a deep distrust of the Passaic River, where he was taken for exercise while we were in Rutherford. He did not object to being near it, for he delighted in browsing along the bank, nosing the mud for insects. Here, again, something had gone seriously amiss with his breeding. Birds neither attracted nor bothered him. Bugs were Bo's prey. But whenever he became aware of the river, he would stiffen, retreat a few steps, and bark at it in anger. The passage of a tugboat, though, would entrance him and he would follow it along the river bank, barking in delighted wrath. But when he saw the wake swelling out and the waves breaking against the black mud shore, he would brake to a frantic halt, snorting and snuffling as his snout plowed the earth—suddenly reminded that he had forgotten about the river.

Still, we hoped that Bojangles would learn to stop embarrassing nature in this manner, and the first summer that he came to the lake with us, I tried to teach him how to swim.

Pulling him down to the water by a leash was a spectacular failure and might have ended in strangulation. He braced his forefeet and refused to budge. I picked him up and carried him out on the dock. He squirmed free. But he fell in the water. Well, I thought, surely nature will take over now. Some atavistic aquatic streak in him will come alive in his brain and guide his feet in a doggy paddle. Surely, faced with the life-or-death alternative of sinking or swimming, a cocker spaniel will swim. Bojangles sank.

There was the last pitiful sight of his pleading eyes and then his black nose and then he was under. I jumped in and pulled him out. Never again did Bojangles go into the water, except once on a very hot day when the lake had coughed up a dead sunfish on the shore. Perhaps drawn by the stench of the fish, he risked the discomfort of a few inches of wetness to examine it with his nose—scurrying quickly back to land where he stood barking at the bloated sunny in a mixture of anger and triumph.

Bo's distaste for water seemed to embrace any creature that dwelt in or on it, and for Lake Erskine's swans he reserved a special enmity.

If they approached the dock, where one of us threw bread crusts to them, Bojangles stood on shore growling in unflinching hostility. When they glided away, the brave Bo occupied the dock and filled the air with the noise of his defiance. Should they veer about and make for him, hissing ominously, their bold challenger became transformed into a flat black streak of retreating cocker spaniel.

For all of his reluctance to act like a dog, we were fond of Bojangles and defended his reputation by explaining that he actually wanted to be a cat. Bojangles was slavishly devoted to Snoopy, the last of our cats and a most superior creature. Snoopy carried himself with a splendid disdain that must have been wounding to Bojangles in its suggestion that Bo was a member of the lower classes. Poor Bo, he tried to copy Snoopy and befriend him. But his surrender to snob appeal brought him constant, painful rebuff.

Whenever Bojangles sighted Snoopy in the house, he yelped happily and ran toward him. Up went Snoopy's tail and back went his lips. Bojangles braked to a skidding halt and reached out a tentative, friendly paw—a copy-cat once again in his very imitation of a feline's use of its legs. His head lolled sideways and he gazed at Snoopy in a pathetic eagerness that seemed to plead,

"Aw, c'mon—don't be stuck-up. There's plenty of room here for both of us."

Snoopy's reply was a fast right hand. While Bojangles reared back, rejected, again pawing the air clumsily, Snoopy moved to a throw rug in the middle of the floor to anchor himself there. Bojangles yelped and rushed. Snoopy side-stepped and swung. Skidding frantically on the smooth flooring, Bojangles slid past the rug like a boat missing its mooring and received a series of sharp blows on his behind. It was unequal combat, but it was repeated frequently, and Bojangles never realized how Snoopy was outwitting him by seizing the solid underfooting of the rug, like a firm island set in the center of that slippery sea of wood.

Bojangles was an individualist. Even when we attempted to teach him tricks, he continued to exhibit that dogged refusal to be pressed into any mold. He could be taught to walk erect, providing that someone held his front paws for him. He could be coaxed into leaping over an outstretched leg, if the rewarding morsel of meat was held in plain view of his eyes and within range of his nose. But try it without the meat, and Bojangles grew bored.

No dog was more affectionate. His front-door welcomes were wet and warm tumults. If he was in the house and heard the door open, he would race for the hall and hurl himself with happy yelps upon the homecomer. He hated to be banished from the company of the family, and when he was let indoors, he ran from chair to chair, snorting and drooling, leaping into every lap to bestow a lick of fondness on every cheek. It distressed him to hear a quarrel. He lay down, whimpering, with his nose between his paws, his floppy ears drooping in dejection. It seemed as though he was trying to cover them with his paws. Sometimes we teased him by pretending to be angry with one another, pushing one another while Bo ran around and around in a frenzy of dismay—leaping in between us to wag his entire rump in an exaggerated display of the friendship which he bore us, as though hoping to shame us out of our spat.

Poor Bojangles, he also drank. It was not a vice of which we were aware until we had grown older and there were frequent parties on the porches either in Rutherford or at the lake. If Bo was outside, he would clamor stridently for admittance, once he had heard the footsteps moving to the refrigerator in the kitchen. Admitted, he did not burst in upon the company with all of that foolish, impulsive explosion of love. He carried himself as correctly as Snoopy and made himself comfortable at someone's feet. If Bojangles drank, he drank like a gentleman.

He waited until a glass of beer had been thoughtlessly deposited on the floor. While the possessor of the glass was occupied in conversation or lighting a cigarette, Bojangles quietly lapped up a few ounces.

"Hey, what happened to my drink?"

"You drank it, silly."

"I did not! It was full a minute ago. I just put it down to light a cigarette."

"You're dreaming! Who would want to take your beer? There's plenty more in the icebox."

During such moments of mystery, Bojangles, sensing exposure, softly wiggled back under chair or sofa, only coming out when the matter had been forgotten and another unguarded beaker had been placed on the floor. He must have been wise enough not to overdo it, patient enough to lap up as much as he might without nosing too deeply into the glass—for he never knocked one over. He was only found out when his unusual decorum drew suspicion down on him, when the cries of, "Hey, what happened to my drink?" became too frequent, and when it was observed that Bojangles, on the mornings-after, was displaying traits of torpor and irritation that were the unmistakable symptoms of hang-over.

One night, someone exclaimed, "Hey, what happened to my drink?" and someone else gasped and said, "I'll bet I know. I'll bet it's Bojangles!"

It was. He was found beneath the sofa, feigning sleep —unaware of the froth of the lager that rested on his nose and whiskers in damning bubbles.

Quick to make himself one of the family, Bojangles swiftly adopted the distinguishing trait of rebelliousness. He slept at the foot of beds where he was not supposed to sleep, he chewed on blankets or shoes not intended for his jaws—and he chewed gum. All of us were forbidden to chew gum, although everyone did—and so did Bo. There was a rich mine of used gum beneath the dining-room table and chairs. It had been hastily plastered there at the moment of Foddy's appearance at the table, and then forgotten. Bojangles' build was admirably suited to getting at this gum. During meals, we could feel him moving softly under table and chairs, sniffing for it and then, finding it, gnawing it free.

"Marion, what is that dog doing under the table?"

Bojangles gave the answer. He would duck under the white tablecloth at the end of the table furthest from Foddy. His jaws would be working in quick, choppy movements of joy, while he snorted and snuffled, shaking his head to free his snout of sticky, crisscrossing cobwebs of gum.

"Lord, what a family!" Foddy would shout. "See how their manners are reflected in the conduct of this poor black beast."

15

The Pink Fairy

The summer of 1937 was our last at the lake. After it, Foddy sold the log cabin. By then, everyone but me had been graduated from high school, and I was in my last year. Elizabeth was training to be a nurse and Madelon studying to be a teacher. The older girls were going through the motions of going to business, while actually engaged in the more important pursuits of courtship, and soon they would begin to marry. No one seemed to care much for the lake any more, so Foddy sold the place.

Betty was married that fall. There was a reception at home, with more than enough champagne. Early in the festivity, I removed two bottles of bubbly from the icebox and stowed them carefully in the garage, guarding against the moment when the party would end and I might retrieve them, to exchange them in an East Rutherford bar for two quarts of Green River whiskey, not less than two months old. The stuff was raw, but it had the virtue of lasting longer than champagne.

The following summer, Catherine married, and the swap was repeated, though by then my sense of values had been sharpened by a year of trading and I was able to negotiate three Seagrams for two Piper Heidsiecks. A month or so later, John married. Here, there was no opportunity to raid the icebox, since the reception was the responsibility of John's in-laws.

Now, there were many empty chairs at the dining-room table, and there came another drop when Marion became ill and was taken to the hospital, when Uncle Tom departed to teach in Washington, and when Elizabeth also married. Only Madelon and I were left, and I, too, would be absent if Foddy could get me a scholarship to Fordham. But I had been no student, and Fordham rejected me.

I thought for a time that I might be accepted by N.Y.U., but when the notion was broached to Foddy, he said, "You want to go to college? What for, Robert?"

Rather than attempt to defend an indefensible position, I let the matter drop and went to work, by days in a factory, by nights on a newspaper, until I had saved enough money to enroll at N.Y.U. But formal education and I were ever incompatible, and I left school to return to newspapers, and then came December 7, 1941.

I had been playing basketball that Sunday afternoon. Returning home, I found Mother and Foddy and Madelon in the library, gathered around the radio. Madelon said, "The Japs just bombed Pearl Harbor."

That night I sought to enlist in the Marines, but I had to wait until January 5, 1942, until I had had an operation performed and the Marines would accept me. And then, the war.

Three years later, in December of 1944, I came back home from the Pacific. Foddy and Mother were on the sidewalk to greet me when I stepped out of the taxicab. Both of them smiled in joy, and Mother, who had injured her leg in my absence, was so excited that she forgot to limp. She only remembered her affliction when I had gotten into the house and embraced Madelon, and Elizabeth, who had come home to live because her husband had been captured by the Germans in North Africa.

On the porch was a huge wicker hamper filled with Rhine wine.

"All yours, Robert," Foddy said grandly. It was. It was also symbolic of the nine months between that moment and the end of the war. The old house came alive again. It rocked to laughter and argument and song and the old piano shuddered beneath the impact of exuberant fingers playing unfamiliar songs. "I've Got Sixpence," "Waltzin' Matilda," "I Don't Want to Be a Soldier," "Bell-Bottom Trousers"—what manner of melody was this? What had happened to "The Minstrel Boy" or "O'Donnell Abu!"?

An astonishing liberality in furloughs brought me home frequently, and when I was there, my married sisters and John would come to the house. There would be new nieces and nephews—born during my absence—to be dandled and admired. The dining table was full again. Mother exhausted her red ration stamps obtaining the roasts of beef which were Foddy's specialty. There was always wine, and there was always company.

Many of our friends in uniform were home, then, and they readjusted quickly to the old custom of having a party at our house. Foddy's liquor supply ran bravely abreast of the demand, for he delighted in filling the glasses of these young warriors and listening to their war stories. But the old scornful wit could come flashing forth again.

A few months before my home-coming, a terrible thing had happened in Yankee Stadium. Army had defeated the Notre Dame football team by 59 to 0. To Foddy, it was almost as black an event as Pearl Harbor. For once, he could not blame the officials or accuse the Army of having twelve men on the field. One night I came home with a friend, an Army lieutenant who had played end for West Point in that game. I introduced him.

"He played for Army last fall, Foddy."

Foddy growled, "Poison him," and left the room. But he came back smiling, laughing at the puzzled expression on the young man's face and brandishing a bottle of Scotch. "Just a little joke," he explained. But he added grimly, "Wait till the war's over."

And in September of 1945, it was over. Yet, it would be another year before the excitement of those stimulating times would begin to subside. More young men were coming home on discharge and had to be greeted and partied. Elizabeth and her daughter were still with us, awaiting the release of her husband from a prison camp in Poland which had been liberated by the Red Army. So the dining table remained crowded, with family and friends—and into this rejuvenation of the old happy time walked Annie.

Annie was perhaps the only cleaning woman who ever got along with Mother. She worked for her one day, when only Mother was in the house. A week later, she made a voluntary reappearance, but one that was intended to be permanent.

A taxicab from Newark appeared alongside of the house. Annie got out, and after her came a perspiring cab driver, unloading the back seat and trunk, crammed with Annie's possessions. There were stacks of cooking pans and basins, boxes of Tintex dye, a tool chest, two or three pairs of pink canvas sneakers, a suitcase full of long cotton dresses of the Mother Hubbard vogue—all dyed pink—a pink bathrobe, a carton of breakfast cereal, a Gideon Bible, an ancient portable sewing machine, a table radio and several cigar boxes containing lipsticks, rouge, powder, compacts, mirrors and bobby pins, and whatever other cosmetics that were required to justify Annie's right to the name which Foddy immediately bestowed upon her. He called Annie the Pink Fairy.

Not even Mother dared to intercept Annie as she marched up the back steps—her feet in their pink canvas sneakers barely visible beneath her trailing pink dress—and harshly directed the driver to place the pots and pans and the boxes of dye in the laundry and to cart the remainder of her things up to the attic. Annie said nothing to Mother, but the confidence of her movements was eloquent of her determination to stay. Having been here once before, she knew the layout. She wasted no time with the cabbie. When he had finished, she paid him and walked into the kitchen.

She began to prepare the evening meal.

"But, Annie," Mother expostulated, "I didn't send for you."

"I came, anyway," Annie said.

"But, what are you doing?"

"Cooking."

"But, Annie, we can't afford a cook. I just wanted you to come one day a week to clean."

Annie replied that it was too much bother riding buses back and forth from Newark, and besides, there was plenty of room in the attic. "Where do you keep the butter?" she asked. Mother motioned weakly to the icebox. She made a final, despairing defense of her propriety. "What are you going to cook?"

"You'll see when you eat it."

Well, none of us could ever equal Annie's assurance in this delicate matter of identifying the dinner. But neither did anyone, even Foddy, dare to badger her for hints on it.

Madelon and I were choking with mirth when Mother left Annie in grim possession of the stove and came into the library.

"Who is she, Mother?"

"Her name's Annie."

"So I gathered," Madelon said. "But where did she come from?" Mother moved her shoulders in a helpless negative and replied, "She says she's going to stay."

"Oh, boy!" Madelon grinned. "Wait till Daddy sees her."

He saw her that night. He was sitting at the head of the table, drumming his fingers irritably while waiting for his dinner. He seemed about to shout at Mother to get on with it, when the swinging doors swung inward and Annie entered. The sound of drumming ceased and there was a horrified silence.

"Good Lord!" Foddy breathed. He lowered his head, watching her warily from the corner of his eyes. Annie placed a container before him. He closed his eyes and shuddered. He did not open them until Annie had gone.

"Marion," he said, "what was that?"

"Oh, pipe down. She's going to stay here and help me."

Foddy placed both hands on the table, leaning back in his chair and lifting his face to the Almighty in a typical what-have-I-done-to-deserve-this appeal. He might have roared refusal, had not Annie again barged through the swinging doors. He glared at her. She met him eyes-on, for the wispy Annie, a woman in that indeterminate age of life which might be anything from forty-five to sixty, was no faint-hearted frail. Her little blue eyes glittered with the concentration of dislike which half of woman-kind bears for the dominant male. The blue of her eyes seemed to be made bolder by that otherwise perfect background of pink—the pink sneakers and long pink dress, the pink-painted fingernails and the pink-dyed hair, the rouged cheeks and dangling pink earrings. Foddy coughed and glanced in distaste at another container which she set before him.

"What's this?"

"Dinner."

His eyes started as he recognized the dish for one of the enameled white metal fruit-and-vegetable trays from the refrigerator. The bottom of it was blackened.

"Lord, woman, you're not cooking in these things, are you?"

Ignoring him, Annie turned to me. "Eat your dinner, dearie, I made it especially for you."

Madelon and Elizabeth giggled and Foddy sought to recoup his failing prestige with a joke. He said to Annie, "Did any member of your family ever have relations with the characters in *Alice in Wonderland?*" Annie gave him her back and said to Mother, "Don't mind him, dearie, I'll take care of you." Mother smiled. She was beginning to enjoy Annie. "That will be all, Annie," she said grandly.

Only a slight inclination of the head gave proof that Annie had heard. She glided from the room and we could hear her rattling dishes in the kitchen and then the soft patter of her feet on the back stairs. She was taking dinner to Bojangles. It was, as it would always be, the choicest bit of meat, served on a good dish. Annie was fond of Bo.

We began discussing Annie in excitement until Foddy pushed his plate away and arose and said to Mother, "Marion, I am going upstairs to rest, and when I return, I will expect to find that that Pink Fairy has flown away."

But when he returned, he discovered that Annie, far from having spread her wings and taken off, had cleared the table and put everything away, had cleaned the kitchen as it had not been cleaned in some time and had gone up to the attic to retire. We heard a muffled pounding up there. I raced up the stairs to investigate. The door of her room was closed, and I shouted to make myself heard above the racket of her hammer. It opened cautiously, and when Annie saw me, she smiled. "Hello, dearie."

There was a big nail driven halfway through the edge of the door. Annie was nailing herself in for the night.

"Annie," I said, "you shouldn't do that. There's a key in the lock. You can lock the door if you want to."

She shook her head and hefted the hammer in her hands. She smiled again, displaying neat pink gums. "I trust you, dearie," Annie said. "But I'm not taking any chances with that ol' man down there."

In the morning, Foddy suffered his second straight defeat. Annie rose early, yanked the nail from her door and pattered down to the kitchen to prepare breakfast. Foddy came down and saw Annie standing grimly in front of the stove. Three or four frying pans of all sizes were filled with sizzling bacon. Annie cooked everything by the pound.

"Lord, woman," Foddy shouted, "you've got enough bacon there to feed a battalion." He moved to rescue it, but Annie raised a menacing spatula and Foddy retreated to the breakfast nook. For the duration of the Pink Fairy's service with us, Foddy and Annie competed for the stove. Foddy would hear Annie stirring about on the floor above and leap from his bed and dash to the bathroom. The sound of her prying the big nail free spurred him through his bath, whooshing and blowing in a panic of haste. Cursing and howling with pain, he would shave and struggle into his bathrobe to dash down the hall and clatter down the stairs to forfend against the infuriating prospect of finding that silent but speedy pink wraith encamped in his kitchen. Madelon and Elizabeth and I kept a running score of this continuing contest. Though we were never on hand to judge who had flashed across the tape—the winner, it was easy enough to tell from Foddy's plate. If his breakfast was left uneaten or only partially consumed, Annie had carried off the palm. If his plate was clean, to Foddy had gone the laurels. Though Annie had led at the start, it is to Foddy's credit that on the day of her departure he had overtaken the Pink Fairy and might have flown out in front.

We had wondered why Annie had brought the boxes of Tintex with her and how she managed to arrive at that pink shade of hair. But in a few days, both questions were answered when I found the Pink Fairy bent over the laundry tub, soaking her head in bright red water. Probably, Annie intended to be a flaming redhead, but though Tintex might impart that color to clothing, it could do only half the job with Annie's hair.

Annie was remarkably energetic. She charged through the rooms with dustcloths and mop and bucket, and routed dust. She took rooms apart and rearranged them to suit her own taste. Not content with the heinous crime of washing Foddy's reading cap, she refused to leave it in its proper place—askew on his bed poster—but put it away in a different drawer every day. Washing and ironing were twin passions, and in satisfying the first, Annie needed but a week to devour Mother's cache of the soapflakes that were then in short supply. Though Mother wearied of scouring the stores for the flakes that would feed Annie's insatiable lust for soapsuds, the Pink Fairy would not hear her complaints or explanations. In ironing, Annie was equally exuberant. To Annie, a garment was not fit to wear unless it was so stiff with starch that it might march off the ironing board. She seemed to think that an occasional scorch mark was only proof of her enthusiasm. When Foddy and I began to take our shirts out to be done, Annie took it as a personal insult and raided the hampers in search of soiled shirts.

Annie despised books. "Dust-catchers," she called them, eyeing the loaded bookcases with unmitigated loathing. She had to be restrained from washing the covers—as she had to be discouraged from bathing the telephone in disinfectant—and it was not uncommon to see the Pink Fairy seated on the floor, surrounded by books, vigorously polishing them with a dustcloth while grumbling direfully to herself, "Books . . . ol' books. . . ." Mother's plants, of which there were many, also enraged her. She insisted on banishing them to the front porch, explaining to Mother that they gobbled up all of the oxygen in the air.

"That's why you're so sickly, dearie," she said sweetly. It made no impression on Annie when Mother replied that she would prefer inhaling weakened air to the daily ordeal of carting her plants in from the porch. Mother, of course, was not sickly, but Annie could not be dissuaded from this conviction. If the plants were not at fault, then, obviously, it was "that ol' man."

"Why don't you leave him, dearie?" she would ask Mother.

It was in cooking, though, that all of the Pink Fairy's redoubtable energy and enthusiasm emerged in awesome splendor. Though we had needed but a week to inure our palates to the taste of enamel which lingered in the food after it had been removed from the refrigerator trays, we were quite baffled in devising a nomenclature for Annie's dishes.

"What is this, Marion?"

"I think it's the lamb I bought today."

"Yes, yes. That is quite possible. But what is this?"

"Oh, heavens, did she cook that, too?"

"Cook what?"

"The liver I bought for Bojangles."

There was always dessert, for the Pink Fairy baked like the good fairy.

"Have some more cake, Foddy."

"Heavens! Was that *cake?*"

Only an empty refrigerator could soothe Annie's driving spirit. A full one, or a partially filled one, seemed to distress her. She spurned margarine and she used more butter than a French chef preparing sauces. Nor could anything be hidden from her. She ferreted it out grimly and threw it into the enameled trays, by now crusted and black on the bottoms.

Annie was convinced that Madelon and I were honeymooners.

"Hello, dearie," she would lisp when I came into the kitchen. "Your sweetheart just went down to the store for me."

"But, Annie, she's my sister."

"Don't kid me, dearie. I saw you two kissing in the front room the other night."

Okay, Annie, have this one your way, too.

Some nights, when the sound of the Pink Fairy's hammer had signaled her retirement from the field, Foddy would call a conference at the dinner table.

"We've got to do something about this, this Pink Fairy, Marion."

"Oh, she's all right. She's just eccentric."

Drawing his breath in determination, Foddy would say, "Euphemism, Marion, does not necessarily lead to optimism. The woman's a nut!"

"Oh, Daddy!"

"Silence, Madelon, I have a theory about this woman. She's been a cook at one time or another." He smiled faintly to himself. "Perhaps in some previous incarnation, she was a cook in a restaurant or a boarding house. More likely a boarding house. That is why she cooks everything in sight. This morning, for example—two pounds of *sassage*. She cooked every one! Last week she took that beautiful ham and cut off a few ham steaks and gave the rest to Bojangles." Foddy's voice rose insistently. "You see what I mean. She's a nut, in the first place, and after that, she's been a cook in a boarding house. She thinks this is a boarding house! That's why she nails herself in at night. That's why she believes that Madelon and Robert are honeymooners. That's why"—

a shrug of injured dignity—"that's why she thinks that
I am—"

"Nonsense," Mother cut in. "That's not it at all. Poor
thing, she's just had her life ruined by some man. See
how she goes on about men? Why, she's forever telling
me that I ought to get rid of you."

Foddy cleared his throat warningly, and Madelon said,
"You're both wrong. Doesn't anyone ever listen to
Annie? It's religious frustration, that's what it is. She's
forever reading that Bible, and she told me once that
she was really a missionary." Madelon's voice was triumphant. "It's religious frustration!"

Theories might analyze Annie, but nothing could explain her away. Only Annie's will would decide whether
she should go or stay. One day, she left. As she had
come, so did she leave. She bundled up her things one
morning—not omitting the mysteriously unused pots
and pans—and called a taxicab from Newark.

"Good-by, dearie," she said to Mother, "I'm going to
be married." She cautioned Mother again to beware of
"that ol' man"—and disappeared. Only the ruined fruit
trays and a few empty boxes of Tintex in the laundry
testified to the reality of the Pink Fairy's six-month
visitation. And we missed her.

16

Run, Louie, Run!

After Annie, the family life ended at 146 Carmita. Elizabeth's husband returned and she moved to her own home and, within a few more months, I had married and moved to Buffalo. In a few more years, Madelon married. Marion was still ill, though eventually she would recover her health, and only Mother and Foddy remained in the big old house. Occasionally, Foddy would suggest that they sell it and take up residence in an apartment. Mother's jaw would come out and she would say, "The only time I'm leaving this house is when they carry me out."

Too many memories anchored her there. Too much of herself and her children spoke from those walls and rooms—not with thin ghostly voices but with robust shouts of laughter to remind her of good times. And it was wise to stay, for where else would she have found room for the families that began to stream homeward on holiday visits? Not infrequently, the upstairs rooms would be filled with sleeping grandchildren and the dining-room table in complete use again.

Foddy would be carving the roast beef and someone else pouring the wine, and someone would be saying, "Remember the time that the electricity meter broke at the lake and we turned on all the lights in the house?"

Foddy would pause. He would frown and say, "I never knew anything about that." Mother would laugh. "Oh, you. You never knew anything that was going on. You were always reading or sleeping." Foddy would shake his head and attack the roast, muttering darkly, "Lord, what a family!"

At last, Mother and Foddy's fiftieth anniversary rolled around and the clan assembled for a party. There were anniversary stories in the newspapers, which gave Foddy's age correctly, but gave none for Mother. She told the reporters, "I'm as old as my little finger and a little bit older than my teeth."

On the morning of the day, a handful of uncles and aunts and cousins joined us for the anniversary Mass. In the afternoon, there was a dinner of roast beef and much bubbly of both colors, followed, at night, by an old-time party in which Betty slid down the banister in defiance of matronly decorum, Foddy danced a jig without losing his trousers and the old piano croaked in delight.

There were eighteen grandchildren present—American Celts in whose veins flowed the blood of Italy, Poland, Switzerland, Germany, England, Scotland, and, dear Lord, it is true, Ireland. Running my eye over that gay gathering, it fell upon Elizabeth flanked by five fair-haired girls and one towheaded boy. Poor Louis Salerno, I thought of my nephew, he's got five sisters, too. I raised my glass and drank to him and he replied with a puzzled grin.

"It's your ball now, Louie," I shouted above the hubbub, "so start running."

ABOUT THE AUTHOR

Before World War II, in which ROBERT LECKIE served with the Marine Corps, Mr. Leckie was a reporter for a local newspaper near his home town, Rutherford, New Jersey, where he still lives with his wife and three children. Mr. Leckie's first book, *Helmet for My Pillow*, was originally written as a novel, but part of the manuscript was accidentally destroyed by a child.

With the disappearance of the novel's first twenty pages, vanished all desire to finish it. Seven years later Leckie started his book again, not as a novel this time, but as his personal narrative of World War II. *Helmet for My Pillow* received the Marine Corps Combat Correspondents Annual Award for 1957.

Formerly the editor of MGM's theater reel, News of the Day, Mr. Leckie is now a free-lance writer. He has had wide newspaper and film experience. His first job was at the age of sixteen, as a sports writer on a New Jersey daily. Since then he has worked on eight newspapers—including some of the biggest in the country—as a reporter, rewrite man, financial editor and copy editor. He has also written documentary films and been editor of *The Telenews Weekly*.

LORD, WHAT A FAMILY!, which goes back to Mr. Leckie's pre-newspaper days, was written in between *Helmet for My Pillow* and a novel.

The novel, which he is now working on, is carefully kept out of the reach of his children. Mr. Leckie reads books on history and philosophy, drinks beer for relaxation, and debates for exercise.